A GUIDE TO CHILD THERAPY:

Let's Play

by

Max Price, Ph.D. and Geri Price

JASON ARONSON INC.
Northvale, New Jersey

A GUIDE TO CHILD THERAPY:

Let's Play

by

Max Price, Ph.D. and Geri Price

JASON ARONSON INC.
Northvale, New Jersey

This book was set in 12 pt. Trump Medieval by Pageworks and printed and bound by Book-Mart Press, Inc. of North Bergen, NJ.

Library of Congress Cataloging-in-Publication Data

Price, B. Max.
 A guide to child therapy : let's play / by B. Max Price and Geri Price.
  p. cm.
 Includes bibliographical references and index.
 ISBN 0-7657-0321-1
  1. Play therapy. I. Title: Let us play.
 II. Price, Geri. III. Title.

RJ505.P6 P75 2001
618.92'891653—dc21

2001022555

Printed in the United States of America on acid-free paper. For information and catalog, write to Jason Aronson, Inc., 230 Livingston Street, Northvale, NJ 07647–1726, or visit our website: www.aronson.com

DEDICATION

To the memory of Max's father, Elmer Price, and his grandfather, Bill Price, who enjoyed playing with children.

To our children, Tracey and Todd, and the joyful memories we have of our playtimes together.

To our daughter-in-law, Pamala, whose playful spirit we admire.

To our grandchildren, Timothy, Jonathan, Elizabeth, and Matthew, with whom we anticipate the continued joy of play.

To Max's child patients, who have shared their hurts, fears, sadness, hopes, trust, creativity, and love in play therapy sessions. We learned much from them.

PREFACE

This handbook contains information I wish had known when I began as a child therapist. It is the sharing of more than twenty-five years of work with children.

This is a practical handbook for play therapists: Students, beginning therapists, and clinicians who desire a handy resource for treating children. The book contains chapters on the use of play therapy in assessing and diagnosing children, conducting a play therapy session, recommended play therapy materials, application of play therapy in treatment of anxiety, depression, behavior problems, separation and loss, violence and disasters. Anecdotal case examples are numerous. The authors' outlook is a multimodal one, which uses play therapy in conjunction with behavior therapy, cognitive-behavioral therapy, parent consultation, and family therapy.

The case examples are taken from actual therapy sessions. The names of the children and specific facts have been altered to protect the confidentiality of my patients.

B. Max Price, Ph.D.
Psychologist

CONTENTS

Preface   v

Acknowledgments   xi

Part I   Basics

1 Let the Play Begin:
Conducting a Play Therapy Session   3

2 Diagnostic Play:
Assessing the Child's Needs,
Developmental Level, and Core Conflicts   19

3 Starting Points:
Basic Assumptions, Uses of Play in
Therapy, Characteristics of an
Effective Play Therapist   37

4 What About Theory?:
The Necessity of Theoretical Orientation,
Theory Applied   51

Part II   Tools of the Trade

5 Basic Play Therapy Materials
Descriptions and Uses   65

6 Therapeutic Storytelling
Mutual Storytelling Technique and
Different Variations   87

Part III   Specific Problems

7 Treatment of Anxiety and Depression   119

8 Treatment of Behavior Problems   141

9 Play Therapy Applied to Separation and Loss:
Divorce, Absentee Parent, Death,
Adoption, Foster Care   173

10 Play Therapy Applied to Trauma and Illness:
Violence, Natural Disasters, Illness   213

Part IV   Behavior Therapy

11 Managing Difficult Behavior in the Office,
School and Community:
Description and Intervention   249

12 Parent Consultation:
for Managing Behavior Problems
Principles, Model, and Example   277

Afterword   **293**

Appendixes   **295**

References   **319**

Index   **321**

ACKNOWLEDGMENTS

I want to thank the following people for helping my idea of writing a play therapy book become a reality. To Geri, for taking the content and "making it interesting."

To our daughter, Tracey Burton, for her hours of preparing the manuscript and being so supportive of her parents' book.

To the psychology doctoral residents at the Oklahoma State Department of Health, who have been responsive to Max's play therapy training seminars. These seminars were the beginning of this book.

To my colleagues: Thomas J. Vaughn, Ph.D., Director of Residency Training, Oklahoma State Department of Health, for his years of partnership, friendship, and encouragement. To C. Eugene Walker, Ph.D., Professor, University of Oklahoma Medical School (retired), for his advice and encouragement in the prospectus development and being so readily available when I asked for consultation. To Vicki Hill, my clinic partner, for her enthusiastic response to the original draft chapters and continued encouragement. To Judy Mee, for suggestions in organization of this book.

Special thanks goes to David Wood, of Jean Barnes Books, who pointed us toward the best publisher for this book. We are indebted to David for information and friendship.

To the staff at Jason Aronson, Inc. who were professional, responsive, available, and eager in the development of the manuscript.

Part I

Basics

LET THE PLAY BEGIN

Conducting a Play Therapy Session

HOW TO BEGIN A PLAY THERAPY SESSION

Four-year-old Marty hesitated as he came to my office door. He stopped and looked around. He didn't respond to my greeting, "Hi, Marty." Instead, his eyes scanned the room, looking for changes in the therapy setting since his last visit.

Marty opened the toy cabinet doors and transformed my office into a play therapy room. He placed cars and trucks on the floor and opened up the playhouse. He put the play telephone on the couch and got the doctor's kit ready. Marty holstered the toy pistol in his back pocket. He concentrated on this serious task without speaking.

My office appeared to be an unorganized collection of toy cars, trucks, police and emergency vehicles, a miniature house, and people. Marty needed the security of finding these same toys in the same place in my office each time he came in. To Marty, the arrangement had purpose; he was ready for therapy.

How do you begin a play therapy session? You need to have a treatment plan in mind based on prior data and diagnosis. But the beginning of a session needs to be based on the child's initial mood and behavior. Begin where the child is: Quiet, loud, happy, sad, frightened, defiant, or cooperative.

Marty was a sad and frightened child who needed a predictable world and one in which he had some control over his life. He needed a therapist on whom he could depend. That's why I first made sure Marty had time to arrange the toys. That's why I began the session as an interested observer who was ready to play with Marty when he was ready.

Much of Marty's young life was chaotic, unpredictable, and scary. His biological mother's severe mental illness often separated him from her and other caregivers. He was living in his third foster home in three years.

Marty was evaluated at the age of three by another psychologist and given a diagnosis of Attachment Disorder of Early Childhood. The report concluded that Marty was an at-risk child for emotional disability and significant developmental delay. He came from a deprived home: His mother had a history of chronic mental illness with a diagnosis of schizophrenia. His maternal grandmother was reported to hallucinate. His father's whereabouts were unknown. For a while, a stepfather provided brief, consistent care.

When I tested Marty, he was functioning at a

three-year, one-month developmental level compared
to his chronological age of four years, four months.
Marty's diagnosis remained the same. He received
speech therapy for language delays. His foster parents and caseworker reported that Marty was fearful
and depressed. Sometimes he regressed to two-year-
old behavior or acted aggressively.

Two of my treatment goals were:

1. To treat Marty's depression through play by rein-
    forcing assertive (not aggressive) behavior and ex-
    pression of his emotions. Marty's caregivers re-
    ported that he reacted to stressful family situations
    by "shutting down emotionally." He withdrew,
    ignored toys, didn't speak, and didn't respond to
    caregivers for an hour or longer. I observed Marty
    in this helpless stance—standing stiffly with arms
    at his side, staring blankly, ignoring toys and his
    caregivers' encouragement for up to fifteen min-
    utes.

2. To provide an atmosphere in which Marty could
    experience joy, wonder, and laughter. His foster
    mother described Marty as a serious child who
    seldom smiled or laughed.

HOW TO ESTABLISH RAPPORT
WITH A CHILD

With Marty, I established rapport by being present to
him and observant of him. I allowed him to express

himself with or without words, responded to his questions, and participated in play on the floor with him. I didn't rush his play.

In this session, Marty spent ten minutes arranging the toys and setting the play agenda. I observed his play and summarized his actions. "You have the cars and trucks lined up. You have the people; there's the Mom, the Dad, the kids—Jack, George, and Carl . . .."

I chose this approach to let Marty know that I was interested in his play and also to model verbal expressions. Marty had been quiet and absorbed in his play. By describing the toy scene, I was suggesting that he talk about his play.

By summarizing Marty's actions, I wanted to describe the order he had created in his play. This young boy's life had been subject to the disorder of unpredictable behavior of his mother and grandmother, frequent changes in his home setting, and his own frightened, sad, and mad moods. I observed that Marty had worked to organize his play therapy. I wanted him to be aware of his accomplishments. My hope was that he would continue to give order and meaning to his play.

I used empathy responses, "Marty, you look happy playing with the people" (family dolls).

Marty complained about one of the foster children in his home, "George got my blue truck and wouldn't give it back."

My response was, "You're mad at George because he grabbed your toys."

Empathy is a powerful gift that therapists can give. I wanted to convey to Marty an accurate understanding of his feelings and the event/situation to which the emotions were tied.

I became more active in his play when Marty invited me with words or body movement such as making eye contact with me, handing me a police car, and saying, "We go put monsters in jail now." "Monsters" was Marty's expression of his fear and anger. He had referred to them in an earlier session. I initiated an action and noted his positive or negative response.

The routine that Marty developed in his first three play therapy sessions continued. I provided sameness, gave him permission to play, attended to his play, and responded to his cues.

HOW TO ASSESS THE CHILD'S TREATMENT NEEDS IN TODAY'S SESSION

Use all the background data you have. Observe the needs that appear to be prominent today and respond to them. Make adjustments based on the child's reactions as the session unfolds.

Early in this session, Marty's need for security was evident. He took two dolls that he called "The Mom" and "The Dad"—his foster parents—and placed them in a car. Marty added his three foster brothers—"The kids. This is Jack, this is George, this one's Carl." Dolls named "Dr. Price" and "Bonnie"—his caseworker—made up his security family. Without my prompting, Marty presented his perception of his world. Marty's play said, "I need adults and siblings near to care for me."

Next, Marty checked the couch to see if "the monsters were still in jail." In earlier sessions, Marty's play demonstrated fear and anger; he said a "monster will get the children." Moving from this helpless and passive behavior in his first session, Marty took a more assertive role in sessions two and three. He identified a male doll as the monster, "put the monster in jail," and shot it with the toy gun. Marty repeated this activity several times.

Today, Marty checked the miniature house, then the couch and said, "the monsters are still in jail." In previous sessions, Marty called policemen to put out a fire. Today, Marty got out a police car and fire truck to protect himself.

In this session, Marty's fears were low. The monsters were not a threat, and he did not have to battle them since he felt emotionally secure.

Marty needed a safe setting in which to assert himself, exercise control of his world, and connect with his therapist. He talked as he played, often giving me directions as I sat on the floor with him. Marty was assertive in his play and decisive in what he wanted to do.

He took a car, gave me one, and announced, "We're going to work." The two of us went off throughout the office and away from the playhouse. Marty demonstrated a normal separation experience without anxiety. As long as Marty's behavior met his needs and was within normal limits, I permitted and encouraged his assertive play.

This behavior was desirable. It met my treatment goal of fostering assertive behavior and expressing both positive and negative feelings.

HOW TO GIVE STRUCTURE, SET LIMITS, AND ALLOW FREEDOM

Children quickly let you know what they need, so I begin with a routine that the child can expect every time. The office is arranged the same way for each visit. I tell the child, "I have two rules. One, you may not hit, kick, or spit. And I won't hit, kick, or spit either. Two, put away the toys you have out before you get any more." Knowing what to expect allowed Marty freedom to act within that structure. He began to feel safe. Marty needed a clear structure to begin, then he could have freedom to explore and express himself.

Marty was a shy, depressed child who needed permission to be assertive and to express his emotions. He needed little limit setting or redirection. Physical aggression or destructive play would indicate that stricter limits were needed. The security of sameness in the play room allowed Marty freedom to act out his concerns. He took charge of his cars and trucks. He was active and verbal as he led our play time. Today, monsters were under Marty's control. He had policemen and firemen available to help him.

Marty stopped playing several times to seek out a new toy, and asked me, "What is this? Where did you get this?" His questions expressed curiosity, wonder, and the energy to explore. I interpreted this play as productive, not a way of evading therapy issues. Marty was more relaxed, playful, and comfortable in conversation with me when he engaged in "exploring and wonder play." His foster mother reported that Marty smiled at home the past two weeks. And, he smiled several times in this session.

Marty volunteered, "I went to a Christmas party." He shared with me a happy time and described what he did at the party. He said, "I choosed and I got a butterfly balloon. I still got it." It was neat to see Marty express some joy in his life.

I set limits on two occasions in this session. During play, Marty went to the cabinet, opened the drawer, and took two pieces of candy from the jar. I reminded him, "You can have candy after you put away your toys." Marty stared at the candy and started to put it in his pocket.

I used a firm voice, pointed at the candy and then at the desk. "Marty, just one piece of candy. Put the other one back in the jar, and leave your candy on the desk." He hesitated and frowned at me, but complied and didn't test this limit again. Marty accepted this limit as a part of his treatment.

Marty complied with the second limit by putting away the toys at the end of the session.

HOW ACTIVE SHOULD THE THERAPIST BE?

Active enough to initiate issues and passive enough to let the child respond genuinely. By the middle of this session, Marty was comfortable enough to engage in conversation with me. He asked me questions.

Holding up a toy crane he asked, "What is this? Will you help me find my white truck?"

I took a more active role in conversation and play. He answered my questions.

"What are the monsters doing?"

"They're in jail."

"Why is George (Marty's foster brother) in jail?"

"He took my toy."

Marty and I played with cars. I asked, "Where are we going?"

Marty replied, "To McDonald's." He visited his biological mother, with supervision, at McDonald's the previous week.

I interpreted this as a significant statement. I wanted to know Marty's reaction to the time spent with his mother. Was it a happy, fun experience? Was it an upsetting experience? Would he shut down emotionally or be talkative about the visit?

I decided to pursue the mother-son theme Marty had introduced in his play. The timing seemed right.

When I asked Marty, "Is your Mom at McDonald's?" he indicated "Yes." Marty's behavior abruptly changed from enjoyable to aggressive and disturbed play. A fire started and we needed a toy fire engine to put it out. Marty took the doctor's kit and was mildly punitive in giving me a "shot." Then he took his toy gun and "shot" me, the only time in the session that Marty used the gun. The aggressive doctor's role was in contrast to Marty's earlier gently bandaging my hand and giving me a shot.

Marty's negative reactions suggested that time spent with his biological mother was both desired and upsetting. This behavior was consistent with his caseworker's report of the visits she supervised, and

Marty's behavior in a joint session with his mother a few months later.

His biological mother's mental illness made it difficult for her to respond appropriately to his needs. At the later visit, I saw Marty change from smiling and playful to quiet, scowling, and withdrawn after she came into the room. The mother acted like a teenager, focusing on herself more than on her son. She was unable to decipher Marty's moods or needs. She held him like a small child. He regressed to a two-year-old level, crying and using toddler language.

I did not correct Marty's aggressive play when he pointed a toy gun at me and said, "I'm gonna shoot you." He gave me repeated "shots" with the play doctor's kit and said, "I'm gonna give you another shot." He participated in loud, excited play with the fire engine, going "Vroom! Vroom! Vroom! Get the fire out." This behavior was a valid expression of his emotional reaction to family visits. And it was important for him to express these emotions—one of my treatment goals.

HOW TO END A SESSION

Goodbyes were difficult for Marty. He needed time to prepare for the session to end. To help him get ready, I said, "We have five minutes before the bell rings, and then it will be time to put the toys away." Marty was reluctant to stop playing. I provided structure through verbal prompts and gestures to encourage him.

"The bell went off. It's time to tell everybody 'bye and pick the toys up." I pointed to the cars and held the toy bin for him. "Put the big car in here. Can you put the toy box in there?" I asked as I pointed to the bookcase.

Marty needed few limits. I helped him pick up the toys and praised him for his good work. The closing ritual was important, "When you finish your job, you can have one piece of candy."

Today, I knelt beside Marty ready to tell him "'bye." As he left, Marty volunteered, "Goodbye." It was a successful ending.

When a child initiates a goodbye hug, I usually accept it. When I hug a child, I prefer for a parent to be present. If a child has been abused, I am reluctant to hug him. If it is a girl patient, I hug or touch on the shoulder only in the presence of a parent.

I do believe in the value of touch. My goal is to encourage healthy touch between child and parent.

Marty was reluctant to touch or be touched. He was not a hugger but he responded to playing close to me. In later sessions, Marty was able to give me brief hugs in the presence of his foster parents.

This session with Marty is an example of how I use play therapy, and the issues I address.

HOW TO INCLUDE PARENTS AND CAREGIVERS

Parent consultation is a part of the child's treatment. With a child as young as Marty, consultation is a necessity. I check with the parent/caregiver at the beginning of each session to see if there is any information I need. Every second or third time, I include ten to twenty minutes alone with parents.

Marty's foster parents brought him to therapy and his caseworker was available for phone and office consultation. The foster mother and father were skilled in parenting and responsive to my suggestions regarding Marty's care. They told me about Marty's behavior each week, of changes in his environment, and visitation times with his biological mother and grandmother. Without such cooperation, Marty's treatment would have been less successful. Unless I have regular contact and consultation with at least one parent/caregiver, I know treatment progress will be difficult.

With school-age children I also provide parent consultation. I explain confidentiality to the child and to the parents. We discuss Informed Consent together so that the child and parents know I will let the child have private time with me within ethical and legal limits.

I tell the child in the presence of her parent(s), "Therapy will be your special time in which you can talk about anything that bothers you. Most things you tell me will be private but there are some things I won't keep private. If I am concerned that you might hurt yourself or someone else, I will tell your parents. If you begin to use drugs or drink alcoholic beverages, I will tell your parents. If I have to go to court, I will not be able to keep our conversations private." I ask the child's parents to agree that this is okay with them. The parents read the Informed Consent and sign it and then I give them a copy. (See the Appendix for a sample of Informed Consent.)

When parents need modeling and training in how to communicate with their child, understand their child's needs and/or set and enforce limits, I include parents in some play therapy sessions. They observe child-therapist interaction, and I give them assignments to practice. In Marty's therapy, parent consultation in every second session was effective.

PRACTICAL EXERCISE

1. Choose one:
   - Review a recent video/audio tape of a play therapy session you had with a child.
   - Review a recent play therapy session using your case notes and observations about the session.
2. Evaluate your performance during the session by checking the appropriate rating.

Self-Rating Checklist

	P	F	G	E*
• Beginning of session	___	___	___	___
• Rapport with child	___	___	___	___
• Child's needs assessed	___	___	___	___
• Today's treatment plan	___	___	___	___

*P = Poor; F = Fair; G = Good; E = Excellent

	P	F	G	E
• Appropriate structure provided	—	—	—	—
• Appropriate freedom and/or limits provided	—	—	—	—
• Therapist's activity level	—	—	—	—
• Ending of session	—	—	—	—
• Parent/caregiver consultation	—	—	—	—

3. Optional:

   Have a colleague or supervisor evaluate your video audio tape using the same rating checklist.

Supervisor's Rating Checklist

	P	F	G	E
• Beginning of session	—	—	—	—
• Rapport with child	—	—	—	—
• Child's needs assessed	—	—	—	—
• Today's treatment plan	—	—	—	—
• Appropriate structure provided	—	—	—	—
• Appropriate freedom and/or limits provided	—	—	—	—
• Therapist's activity level	—	—	—	—
• Ending of session	—	—	—	—
• Parent/caregiver consultation	—	—	—	—

Comments Section

- Strengths of the session: _____

_____

_____

_____

_____

- Weaknesses of the session: _____

_____

_____

_____

_____

- What you learned: _____

_____

_____

_____

_____

- Future plans for treatment of this child: _____

_____

_____

_____

_____

_____

CHILDQUOTE

I Got Problems

Eight-year-old Adam knew exactly why his parents had brought him for therapy. During the first session he told Max, "I have trouble with obedience." In the second session, he said, "Sometime I'd like for you and me to drink a Coke, and just sit down and talk about my problems. I've got a bunch of 'em."

2

DIAGNOSTIC PLAY

Assessing the Child's Needs, Developmental Level, and Core Conflicts

Diagnostic play is a necessary component of the evaluation process. In today's clinical setting, I am likely to see a child for no more than eight to twelve sessions.

So, within the first two or three sessions, I need to make a thorough diagnosis of the child's problems, give accurate feedback and recommendations to the parents, and formulate an efficient plan.

DIAGNOSTIC ASSESSMENT

The following is the model I use.

Background Information

Parents complete an information sheet describing presenting problem(s), the family constellation, developmental history, medical information, academic status, the child's strengths and problem areas, situational stress, and parents' expectations regarding therapy.

Previous Testing

I request copies of any previous psychological evaluations, educational testing, school records, and pertinent medical reports. I ask parents to bring test results with them for the first appointment, if possible.

Diagnostic Interview

I briefly interview parent(s) and child to hear their concerns and observe family interaction. Most of the initial appointment time is a parent interview in which I gather background data, focus on presenting problem(s) and make initial recommendations.

During the parent interview, the child is usually given an assignment of projective drawings: House-Tree-Person Drawing Test, Kinetic Family Drawing, and/or a sentence completion test. The child completes the assignment in a separate room. If the child is too young or frightened to be left alone, she stays in my office and plays with toys while I interview her parents. Through unstructured play or projective drawings, her behavior adds significant data to the assessment process.

Additional Testing

Depending on the child's needs, I may recommend a psychological evaluation, educational testing, a neurological evaluation or referral to a physician for medical evaluation.

Behavior Checklists

I usually include one or more behavior checklists as part of the initial appointment:

The Conners' Parent Rating Scales, Hawthorne Educational Services, Inc., ADDES Rating Forms, and the Child Symptom Inventory.

Diagnostic Play (usually two sessions)

I assess the child's functioning in these three areas:

1. **The child's needs** including the amount of limit setting, structure, freedom, and nurturing needed;
2. **Developmental level** including physical status, cognitive, social and emotional level of functioning, specific strengths, and problem areas;

3. **Core conflicts.** Using the developmental model from the book *From Instinct to Identity* (Breger 1974), I seek to identify which of the developmental conflicts are most significant for treatment.

Author Louis Breger states that as a child progresses through life's stages, certain core conflicts repeatedly appear. "Each (conflict) becomes prominent at a particular time, reaches a peak intensity, is worked through or put aside as another conflict builds, only to reappear in a new form later on" (192–193).

In diagnostic play, I try to assess which conflict(s) are most prominent at this time in a child's life and which conflict(s) need to be the focus of treatment.

Dependence versus Independence

The child seeks to reach some equilibrium between the two extremes of a dependent position of relying upon parents (and other caretaker adults), and the independent position of autonomy, seeking to move away from dependency to do things "by myself," to rely upon her own abilities.

Security versus Anxiety

The child's sense of a safe attachment to parent (caretaker adult), extended family and, in later childhood, to a sense of approval of the social group versus separation anxiety resulting from a sense of abandonment or rejection by parents, significant adults and/or peers. The basic source of this anxiety is helplessness.

Aggression and its Control

This involves the child's expression of aggression from "strong willed," oppositional behavior and resistiveness to parents and authority figures to sibling rivalry and expression of physical attacks on others, versus the internalizing of family and society rules of controlling aggressive impulses and/or finding appropriate outlets for aggression.

The development of conscience and morality are essential components of control of the child's aggressive impulses.

Love versus Hate

This refers to the emotional attachment that the child has to parents and significant adults and peers, versus anger (hate) aroused by abandonment or sense of rejection by the loved person. The anger is related to the anxiety noted in security versus anxiety.

Sensual Pleasure and its Renunciation

This refers to the child's ability to find pleasure and enjoyment in physical contact, i.e., holding, caressing, kissing, and sexual stimulation versus accepting the family's and society's prohibition of unacceptable sexual behavior including incest, premature sexual activity, and sexual assault.

Excitement versus Boredom

This refers to the child's expression of curiosity and interest in finding exciting new opportunities, versus the state of boredom in which the child experiences too much of the same old thing and a lack of stimulating experiences.

I find assessing children in these core conflict areas as extremely helpful for diagnosis and treatment plans.

CASE EXAMPLE ONE—BECKY, SIX-YEAR, TWO-MONTH OLD GIRL

Becky was a girl who was referred to me for grief reactions related to multiple deaths of family members over the past eight months. Her mother died suddenly from a brain aneurysm. Becky's paternal grandfather died two months earlier. Her grief-stricken father reported, "This year has been a black hole for us." The family experienced the death of seven relatives in three years.

Becky's presenting problems included separation anxiety when away from her father and other caregiving relatives, anxiety in new situations and nighttime fears. At school, she frequently behaved in an attention-getting manner and dominated her classmates. Becky talked a lot in class. She interrupted her teacher saying, "Mrs. Jones, I'm already done with my drawing. Look at this." She took the teacher role with other children saying, "Teacher wants us to do it this way. Let me show you how," whether her classmates wanted help or not.

Assessing Needs

Becky walked into my office holding onto her father with her right hand and clutching a stuffed monkey close to her chest. At four-feet-three-inches tall, and 96 pounds, she looked more like a seven- or eight-year-old child. In conversation in her father's presence, Becky alternated between friendly, mature and assertive conversation, and clinging, dependent, regressive speech.

"Dr. Price, can I draw pictures again today? . . . I'll put some apples on this tree and draw a rainbow here . . .. This is my Dad and me going to school . . .. I feed my dog every night . . .. Daddy, help me, I can't tie my shoe . . .. Me don't want to go now."

In diagnostic play, Becky responded well to the dollhouse. She talked as she played with it. Becky demonstrated active, assertive play. "Let's put the bed here; this is the kitchen; this is the kid's room; this is the baby's bed; it's time for them to go to bed."

She spoke of Christmas presents she received and relatives she'd visited. "Guess what, Dr. Price? For Christmas, we went to Gramma's house. I got this sweater, a big dollhouse, and I got a baby bear. We had ham and potatoes and chocolate cake. My Aunt Faye and my Uncle Ralph and my Aunt May and my baby cousin, Kyle—they were all there."

Becky also exhibited dependent play. She became quiet and waited for me to initiate play themes. She regressed in speech, taking the role of the baby doll, saying "Ma-ma, da-da, baby hungry." This regression was particularly noticeable when I mentioned her mother's name.

"Is the mother's (doll) name, Mary?" Becky became very quiet, ignored my question, and hugged Charlie, her stuffed monkey, a gift from her deceased mother.

I used the following rating form to assess Becky's needs:

Table 2–1   Assessment of Needs—Becky

	Low	Average	High	Very High
For Structure			X	
For Limits		X		
For Control			X	
For Freedom		X		
For Security				X
For Emotional Support (nurturing, affection)				X
For Anger Management		X		
For Impulse Control		X		

Parent interviews, background information, and diagnostic play showed Becky's prominent needs were for security and emotional support. She asked for sameness and chose the dollhouse each of the first two sessions using identical play themes. Becky resisted the end of each session, wanting more time. She cried sadly when her father told her it was time to leave.

At home, Becky experienced nighttime fears—awakening several times each night, crying, and calling for her daddy. She once said, "I'm afraid Daddy will leave and never come back," the way her mother left for work and never came home. Becky frequently hugged her monkey, clear evidence of her high need for affection.

In the safe setting of therapy, Becky displayed periods of assertiveness, telling me what she wanted to play, and usually took the teacher or parent role.

"I'll be the teacher, you be the kid.. . . Now, write your letters on this paper.. . . No, I'll show you how to do it."

Assessing Developmental Level

Having a good understanding of child development is essential to assessing developmental level. I used the following chart for Becky:

Table 2–2   Assessment of Developmental Levels— Becky

Chronological Age	6 years, 2 months
Physical Stature	Weight in 95th percentile. Overweight. Size of typical 8-year-old.

Table 2–2 *(continued)*

Cogntive Level	7 and one-half years. High average intelligence. Very verbal. Above average achievement in kindergarten.
Social/Emotional	Fluctuates from advanced (8 years) to regressed (3-year-old-level).

Becky was a bright six-year-old likely to be judged as two or three years older than her chronological age. She attempted to be the strong, assertive older child, but was really a grief-stricken young girl who missed her mother terribly. She was frightened and sad, and wanted to be small again and have someone to take care of her. Her world was full of insecurity and fear, but Becky attempted to cope and be strong.

Table 2–3   Core Conflicts Rating—Becky

	Satisfactory Coping	Minor Conflict	Major Conflict
Dependence versus Independence			X
Security versus Anxiety			X
Aggression and its Control		X	

	Satisfactory Coping	Minor Conflict	Major Conflict
Love versus Hate	X		
Sensual Pleasure and its Renunciation	X		
Excitement versus Boredom	X		

After my parent interview, two sessions of diagnostic play indicated that treatment would focus on security and nurturing, and grief symptoms of anxiety and sadness. Becky's stages of grief would likely fluctuate from periods of denial, strong separation fears and sadness, and periods of coping well by relying on relatives and teachers who were her multiple caregivers.

I expected her to have periods of regression and dependency when she would need to be cared for and protected. There would also be times when Becky would be assertive and controlling. Becky's support group: Father, grandparents, aunts, school teachers, and people at church would be vital to her recovery. Although her physical appearance and cognitive ability were that of an 8-year-old, I wanted adults to recognize that she was a 6-year-old child who was likely to regress and behave as if she were younger.

Becky's treatment plan was developed using diagnostic play assessment, a diagnostic interview with father and child, and background information.

CASE EXAMPLE TWO—MIKE, NINE-YEAR-OLD BOY

Mike was a boy referred to me by his parents and a psychologist colleague for behavior problems at school. Mike lived with his biological parents and twelve-year-old sister. His mother was an educator; his father an accountant. The parents placed a high priority on family life and were active in their local church and community. Mike was an A student in third grade with strengths in athletics and vocal and instrumental music.

Presenting problems included verbal and physical aggression toward peers at school and temper outbursts in the classroom. Prior to his initial appointment, Mike was suspended from school for one day because of a prolonged anger outburst. Mike cursed, hit a classmate, and talked back to his teacher declaring, "He keeps pestering me; he started the fight."

Mike's parents reported that he misbehaved at school beginning in the first grade. Teachers who were strict and ran a structured classroom had less difficulty controlling Mike's behavior. Mike's primary needs were to control his impulsive behavior and anger with his peers.

Assessing Needs

Mike was a healthy, blond-haired boy of average size. He was reluctant to talk about his reason for coming to see me. His father said, "I don't understand why my son is so aggressive. When I was a boy, I was aggressive, but I controlled my anger. Why can't you, Mike?"

Mike defended himself and said, "Ben kept on calling me names during recess. The teachers wouldn't do anything. I stood up for myself."

Mike dropped his head, clenched his fists, and began to cry. His mother put her arm around him and said, "It's all right, son. Dad was just trying to help. We're seeing Dr. Price to help you learn to control yourself."

In diagnostic play, Mike's behavior was in sharp contrast to Becky's. Reluctant to engage in storytelling with drawings, puppets, or clay and animals, he had difficulty using fantasy in his play. Mike was more oriented toward action, choosing competitive games such as *Sorry* and *Carrom* (a pool-type game using wooden rings).

Mike told me, "I like to play all kinds of sports. . . . I wrestle with my dog, and I watch TV shows with lots of action."

Since Mike had difficulty in expressing himself in free play, I used structured activities including projective drawings of the House-Tree-Person Drawing Test, and Kinetic Family Drawing, and the therapeutic board game Talking, Feeling, Doing Game by Richard Gardner. To assist with the diagnosis, I administered the Roberts Apperception Test for Children (RATC).

I used the following form to assess Mike's needs:

Table 2–4   Assessment of Needs—Mike

	Low	Average	High	Very High
For Structure			X	
For Limits		X		
For Control			X	
For Freedom	X			
For Security				X
For Emotional Support (nurturing, affection)			X	
For Anger Management			X	
For Impulse Control				X

Mike's prominent needs were for security and control of his impulsiveness and aggression. Diagnostic play and projective testing, along with the parent interview and background information, indicated that Mike had a moderate degree of behavior and emotional problems. Insecurity and anxiety were primary with anger outbursts and aggressiveness secondary. Mike demonstrated a high need to win in any game situation. He became emotionally upset and frustrated when he was not winning in his game play with me. This competitiveness, along with his fragile ego strength, suggested the need to focus on self-concept and anger management.

Table 2–5   Assessing Developmental Levels—Mike

Chronological Age	9 years, 5 months
Physical Stature	10 years. Average range in height and weight. Well-coordinated for sports activity.
Cognitive Level	11 years. High average. Mike was an A student in third grade.
Social/Emotional	7-to-8 year level. Mike had poor impulse control. His emotions often flooded him. He had frequent peer conflict and sibling rivalry with his achieving and compliant sister.

Mike's physical and cognitive development were average to high average. He had the emotional energy to achieve academically at his intellectual ability level. But, Mike's social and emotional level were below his chronological age, making it difficult for him to succeed with his peers and to measure up to the maturity level his parents expected of him.

Table 2–6 Core Conflicts Rating—Mike

	Satisfactory Coping	Minor Conflict	Major Conflict
Dependence versus Independence			X
Security versus Anxiety			X
Aggression and its Control			X
Love versus Hate		X	
Sensual Pleasure and its Renunciation	X		
Excitement versus Boredom		X	

After two sessions of diagnostic play, projective drawings, and an apperception test (RATC), I concluded that a multimodal treatment approach was needed to address Mike's insecurity and anxiety, low frustration tolerance, anger outbursts, and family conflicts with his parents and sister. The treatment plan would include:

1. Structured play therapy to improve Mike's ego strength, and increase awareness of his emotions and connected events.

2. Family therapy to address Mike's conflict with his father and sibling rivalry with his sister and parent consultation for a behavior management program using a token economy program for school behavior.

3. Anger management and impulse control using cognitive behavioral techniques including relaxation training, guided imagery, and desensitization of anger reactions. With Mike's limited ability to use fantasy, he would respond best to specific suggestions in imagery, and to behavioral rehearsal and role playing for impulse control and frustration tolerance.

4. Social skills training either through a school counselor's group or a play therapy group.

Mike's parents were motivated for treatment and agreed to the multimodal approach. Helping Mike control himself and improve his behavior at school were their main concerns, and they were willing for the entire family to be involved in treatment.

PRACTICAL EXERCISE

Using the format given in the case examples of Becky and Mike, assess a client's behavioral and emotional needs, developmental levels, and core conflicts. See Appendix 2.

CHILDQUOTE

Test Responses

Six-year-old Ted was being tested for learning disabilities. He cooperated for forty-five minutes, attempting to answer all questions, both the easy and hard ones. Fatigued after a difficult question, Ted looked at me and said, "Two things wrong. One, I don't know (the answer). Two, these are *too hard*!"

3

STARTING POINTS

Basic Assumptions, Uses of Play in Therapy, Characteristics of an Effective Play Therapist

Play is the language of children. Haim Ginott (51) stated, "The child's play is his talk and toys are his words."[1]

This is the starting point for a play therapist. To understand a child, I need to spend time in play with her. I can make the mistake of thinking that talking to and reasoning with a child is the best way to communicate. Not true: I begin with play and then I can share my verbal wisdom.

A child's play is her work. Children are unable to verbalize many of their thoughts, feelings, wishes, and fears. In play therapy, toys become the medium

---

[1]Haim Ginott, *Group Psychotherapy with Children*, New York: McGraw-Hill, 1961.

of communication between child and therapist. Until a child is old enough to express her emotions in words, she will speak in her best language: Play.

This chapter contains some basic assumptions about play therapy, uses of play therapy, and characteristics of an effective play therapist.

BASIC ASSUMPTIONS ABOUT PLAY THERAPY

There is Value in Unstructured Play

According to T. Berry Brazelton, M.D., a noted pediatrician at Harvard Medical School, "Play is the most powerful way a child explores the world and learns about himself." [*Time*, November 23, 1998,p. 86.] In unstructured play a child is free to choose what she wants to do, what toys and games to use, and with whom to play within the boundaries of safety and family rules. Such play encourages the development of language, independent thinking, and creativity, and allows young children to negotiate relationships with their peers. When children choose pretend games such as fireman, policeman, house, school, building, or war, they are expressing themselves in a manner and language specific to their age, interests, and concerns.

Despite the value of unstructured play, many children's daily schedules are filled with activities such as individual or team sports, music and dance lessons that, while worthwhile, leave little time for play. Today's children, ages three to twelve, spend only one-and-a-half hours to two hours daily in unstructured play according to a nationwide research project (University of Michigan's Institute for Social Research compiled 1,997 time diaries of 3,586 children, ages twelve and under). [*Time*, November 23, 1998, p. 86.]

Play Therapy is a Specialized Use of Play

Both free play and structured play are used based on the needs of the child and the type of her treatment. Kevin O'Connor states that "the play therapist has two primary responsibilities. First is the creation and maintenance of the therapeutic setting, the relationship in which the work of therapy will occur. Second is the conduct of the work of therapy by first creating experiences that foster the child's development and then helping the child verbally process those experiences so that optimal generalization is effected. Sometimes this means leading the sessions; sometimes this means following the child. Sometimes this means taking a more distant, observing role."[2]

Knowing a Child's Developmental Level Is a Necessity

Therapy is adapted to the child's level whether at low or very high levels of functioning; whether the child has a handicap or is gifted.

---

[2]Kevin O'Connor, *The Play Therapy Primer*, New York: John Wiley & Sons, 1991, p. 99.

Higher Adaptive Functioning is the Goal

The ultimate goal of play therapy is for the child to achieve a higher level of adaptive functioning. An example is Marty as discussed in Chapter One. The goal for Marty was to progress to more autonomy in his life. During a year of treatment, he developed from the two-to-three-year-old level to the four-year-old level.

Most of the children we see in therapy are stymied in their emotional and adaptive development due to life circumstances. When the conditions for growth are present in therapy and in their environment, most children will grow and develop.

USES OF PLAY IN THERAPY

The following is a list of the ways I use play in diagnosing and treating children:

As Part of a Diagnostic Assessment

I use a less structured play time with a child to help assess his or her developmental levels. (Chapter One provides an example with four-year-old Marty.)

1. Social/Emotional Levels.

The child's play helps reveal his social/emotional level. My colleague, Sharon Barton, shared this model based on Piaget's model of cognitive development, Erikson's psychosocial theory, and Virginia Axline's model of play therapy. In a thirty-to-forty-minute play session, I observe the child's play and note which stage he chooses in play.

Stage 1: Win Level. The child chooses an activity and toys that he can control and with which he can win. Often the child engages in solitary play with the therapist as an interested observer and occasional participant.

An example of Stage 1 is the child who plays with a dollhouse, arranging the furniture and people without wanting or asking for the therapist's active involvement. The child prefers solitary play with adults as observers and occasional helpers.

Stage 1 is at the two-to-three-year-old developmental level.

Stage 2: Win/Win Level. The child includes the therapist in the play but both still win. There is no competition or chance the child will lose at this stage. The child manipulates the activity and makes up the rules so he will win and usually so the therapist will win also. There is active involvement and closeness with the therapist.

An example of Stage 2 is a boy who played the game *Candyland* with me. Billy turned all the cards face up so he could pick out the one he needed to win. But Billy quickly did the same with my player and moved it to the end with his player.

Billy declared, "We both win." Stage 2 play is at the four-to-six-year-old developmental level.

Stage 3: Chance Level. In this stage, the child takes some risk. The child chooses a game of chance that usually involves spinning a number, rolling dice, or drawing cards. Stage 3 includes activity in which there is a chance that the therapist will get some power over the child, a chance the therapist may win the game. The child plays by the game rules. An example of this level is the game of *Sorry.* Stage 3 is at approximately the six-to-eight-year-old developmental level.

Stage 4: Skill Level. The child prefers games and activities in which skill plays a part in winning and losing. The Skill level usually occurs when the child has enough ego strength to risk losing, and feels positive about himself. Common games chosen at this level are *Checkers, Chess, Connect Four,* table pool, and sports. While there is some overlap between Stages 3 and 4, the age range is approximately the eight-year-old and above developmental level.

2. Behavioral and Emotional Problems.

In the initial play time, I observe for:

Regression—child engaging in play younger than his or her chronological age, language (babytalk), taking the role of a young child or infant.

Aggression—physical and verbal aggression themes, destructive play.

Fears and Anxiety, Sadness/Depression themes, view of the world as a safe or dangerous place, emotional support available or not available to the child.

3. Needs.

Amount of limit setting, structure, freedom, nurturing needed. Developmental conflicts are assessed. See Chapter Two for checklists for assessing needs.

For Rapport Building

I find supportive play therapy to be an excellent way for me to communicate empathy and acceptance of a child. It is a good way to relate to the child. A play setting quickly communicates to the child that I am ready to enter into the child's world.

With Behavior Therapy

Using play as a reinforcer for talk therapy and for behavior compliance.

Some children are reluctant to talk about behavioral, learning, emotional, or family problems. I have had older children who wouldn't, or didn't know how to, verbalize their pain. Frequent responses to the therapist or parent questions were, "I don't know . . . Yes . . . No . . . " staring blankly, shrugging shoulders or heading for the toys. With such children, I often use these approaches:

"Mike, today we're going to take ten minutes to talk about how well you controlled your hitting and screaming this week. Then, you'll have time to choose what we will play today."

"Susan, you've worked hard today practicing how to face your fears like I asked you. Now you choose today's play activity."

"Doug, we're going to look at your school behavior records for this week. Let's see which things you did well and which things you had problems with. We will practice some at how to control yourself. Play time will be after you finish practice time." If Doug is cooperative, play time begins soon. If Doug doesn't cooperate, little or no play time will be available during that session.

As a Means of Teaching How to Parent

Parents observe as I model effective ways of parenting and interpreting children's play behavior. I include parents in play with their children. Some parents have difficulty relating to children and/or they spend a lot of time correcting, scolding or seeing that daily living tasks are completed. They have little experience in simply nurturing their children. I model play behavior, invite parents to participate, and reinforce them for focusing on their children. Such family play experience can strengthen damaged parent/child relationships.

Specific training for caregivers of young children with significant behavior problems can be effective. The Parent Child Interaction Training (PCIT) is an excellent example. The therapist is behind a two-way mirror and communicates through an earphone to the parent (usually the mother) with her child in the treatment room. Specific, constant directions are given to the parent in managing and relating to her child.

AS A PRIMARY MEANS OF DOING THERAPY WITH PRESCHOOL AND ELEMENTARY SCHOOL AGE CHILDREN

Time and again, I have seen children express themselves clearly in play, gain insight about themselves and their families, and make behavior changes through play therapy which would have been unlikely using talk therapy only. Play therapy is a necessity in work with children.

As a Stress Management Technique for Children

Stress management for all of us focuses on recreation and relaxation activities to cope with daily stressors. Adults and children need to have play as part of their lives. Adult toys (boats, bikes, recreation vehicles, sports, vacations) just cost more than children's toys.

CHARACTERISTICS OF AN EFFECTIVE PLAY THERAPIST

This is my list of basics for effective play therapy.

Knowledge of Child Development

Knowing a child's stage of development, normal and abnormal behavior for each age level, and how to facilitate growth to the next level of functioning is essential.

A Sound Theoretical Foundation

Theory provides a base with which to approach diagnosis and treatment. Without theory, a play therapist can just operate with a bag of eclectic methods and no overall foundation. Most practitioners are eclectic in methods in order to provide the best treatment for different problems. But, effective therapists know the reason they use a particular method, and the theory and research on which it is based.

Ability to Play with Children

Therapists can be so verbal and reason-oriented that they don't know how to get down on the floor and engage children in play. Playing with children is fun! It's a privilege when our work is enjoyable. One kindergarten boy looked up at his mother as we sat on the floor playing together and asked, "Mom, when does Dr. Price have to go to work?"

Belief in the Efficacy of Play Therapy

Experience with children for more than twenty-five years has shown me over and over again how children use play therapy to get better. If you are convinced that play therapy works, you will hone your skills in the use of this powerful treatment modality.

A Good Behavioral Scientist

An effective therapist uses the scientific method in therapy:

Data Gathering—Therapist observes the child and collects information about the child's strengths, needs and problems.

Hypothesis—The therapist develops a professional guess as to the best treatment approach to use.

Hypothesis Testing—The therapist implements the treatment and measures the results (child and family's behavior).

Evaluation—The therapist evaluates the effectiveness of the intervention.

Adjust Hypothesis—Make corrections and adjustments to therapy.

Repeat Process—The therapist continues to adjust the treatment based on the information gained and the child's behavior.

This method is used for both the overall treatment plan and for each session.

Good Facilitation Skills

The play therapist needs to practice the necessary communication skills of empathic understanding, positive regard and genuineness to the child, both nonverbally and verbally. These skills are a prerequisite for an effective play therapist.

PRACTICAL EXERCISE

1. Evaluate your play therapy skills.
   a) Knowledge of child development
      Inadequate ___   Adequate ___   Very good ___
      Plans for improvement:

   b) Theoretical foundation
      Inadequate ___   Adequate ___   Very good ___
      Plans for improvement:

   c) Ability to play with children
      Inadequate ___   Adequate ___   Very good ___
      Plans for improvement:

2. Review a session with your child. How effective were you in using the scientific method?

Inadequate ___   Adequate ___   Very good ___

Plans for improvement:

CHILDQUOTE

Creative Thinking

Seven-year-old John was busily involved in battle scenes during sand tray play one session. He had aggressive animals attacking smaller ones. Earlier the dinosaurs had been defeated by his animals. Continuing his play without any delay, John looked for new enemies. He said, "And the dinosaurs became *inextinct* and attacked these animals."

Wanting To Be Big

Four-year-old Carl wanted to play a table game that was designed for older children. The therapist said, "Carl, you have to be able to count to play that game." Carl immediately said, "I can count." After a short pause, he asked, "What's count?"

4

WHAT ABOUT THEORY?

The Necessity of Theoretical Orientation, Theory Applied

Is there a theoretical basis for what you're doing in play therapy? Are there research results to justify your techniques? These two questions will be on the mind of an effective play therapist as she evaluates her work with children.

Which theory is best for you? There are effective therapists from different theoretical orientations. Psycho-analytic, humanistic, developmental, systems, and cognitive-behavioral are major theories. Various adaptations of these theories have been developed for play therapy. Theories and techniques are well presented in books by Schaefer, O'Connor and James (reference: *Handbook of Play Therapy*, edited by Charles E. Schaefer & Kevin O'Connor, 1983; *The Play Therapy Primer* by Kevin O'Connor, 1991; *Play*

Therapy: A Comprehensive Guide by O'Dessie Oliver James, 1997).

Most play therapists are eclectic in the techniques they use; we want to use those that are effective with a particular child. But a bag of techniques without a sound theoretical basis is like a house with a weak foundation. Treatment will shift back and forth without a clear rationale for what and why you are using these techniques. So, what about theory?

DEVELOPMENTAL THEORY IS A MUST

A child comes to a play therapist because he has regressed or become stuck in one or more aspects of his cognitive, social, behavioral, or emotional development. Therapeutic intervention is designed to free the child from the constraints that hinder his healthy development. The primary work of therapy is to foster that development. Knowledge of developmental stages allows the therapist to recognize the present developmental level of the child and to set therapy goals that will help him move to the next level.

Knowledge of normal developmental stages is basic for any play therapist. If you are working with a six-year-old child, how can you recognize what is abnormal behavior if you don't know what is normal? How can you set effective treatment goals if you don't know the child's developmental level or recognize his developmental needs and conflicts?

The Gesell Institute of Human Development has excellent books on children ages one through fourteen. These books are good resources for parents and therapists. They provide characteristics of each age with suggestions for parenting.

The writings of David Elkind, Erik Erikson, and Jean Piaget are helpful in understanding the developmental stages of children and adolescents.

NECESSARY CONDITIONS FOR THERAPEUTIC CHANGE

Carl Rogers' client-centered therapy helped define the facilitative skills that distinguish the most effective therapists from those who are less effective. The work of Truax and Carkhuff provided a structure for defining, measuring and teaching the skills. The necessary conditions are *empathic understanding, positive regard*, and *genuineness*. These communication skills provide the setting in which a child can make changes.

The work of Rogers, Truax, and Carkhuff was invaluable in my training. If we provide a healthy therapeutic setting, children will respond positively and grow in development. This is consistent with my philosophical belief that children are bent toward positive growth and development. I believe that children will do the work of therapy when the therapist and caregivers provide a therapeutic climate for growth.

However, I disagree with Carl Rogers in his statement that empathy, unconditional positive regard, and congruence (genuineness) are the necessary and sufficient conditions for change. These are necessary but not sufficient, for specific treatment procedures are needed for specific problems. I have found cognitive-behavioral theory and techniques effective in treating children, especially ones with anxiety, depression, social, and behavioral problems.

When treating a child, I ask myself, "What kind of therapy is best for this type of child with this type of problem?"

Having a sound base of developmental theory, communication skills from client-centered therapy, and specific treatments from cognitive-behavioral therapies will equipyou for effective work as a play therapist.

THEORY IN PRACTICE

Using Marty (from Chapter 1), and Becky and Mike (from Chapter 2), here are three examples of theory in practice:

Case Example One—Marty, Four-Year-Old Boy

Marty, in foster care with a diagnosis of Attachment Disorder of Early Childhood and Depression.

Presenting Problem:

Depression exhibited in withdrawal, helplessness, nonresponsiveness.

Treatment Goals:

1. Reduce depression and helplessness.
2. Increase appropriate expression of positive and negative emotions.
3. Foster attachment to therapist.

Theories	*Techniques*
1) Developmental	• Diagnostic testing and diagnostic play to assess developmental delays: cognitive, behavioral, and emotional.
2) Client-centered	• Therapeutic play that demonstrates communication skills of empathy, positive regard, and genuineness to establish rapport and provide a safe setting for Marty.
3) Psycho-dynamic	• Release through play in which Marty expressed his fears, distress, anger and took some control of his world.
4) Behavioral	• Positive reinforcement of assertive behavior through use of attention and praise.

Theories	*Techniques*
	• Positive reinforcement of Marty's including therapist in play to foster attachment.
	• Modeling to provide Marty an example of a nurturing parent figure who expresses emotions in a predictable manner.
	• Consultation with foster parents to use effective parenting techniques in Marty's care.

Case Example Two—Becky, Six-Year-Old Girl

Becky experienced the sudden death of her mother.

Presenting Problems:

Separation anxiety, sadness, and shifts in behavior from regression to aggression.

Treatment Goals:

1. Foster healthy grieving.
2. Reduce Becky's insecurity and separation fears.
3. Provide support and guidance to widowed father.

Theories	Techniques
1) Developmental	• Diagnostic play to assess her developmental levels and needs.
2) Psycho-dynamic	• Play therapy treating Becky's core conflicts of dependence versus independence, security versus anxiety and regression to preschool age. • Grief therapy through play, bibliotherapy, and talk therapy in which Becky could express her profound pain over the loss of her mother. • Therapeutic storytelling with puppets, dollhouse, drawings.
3) Systems theory	• Grief therapy for father and child in family therapy session.
4) Cognitive-Behavioral	• Desensitization training for separation anxiety and fears. • Parent consultation regarding meeting Becky's needs for routine, security, consistent rules, and nurturing from caregivers.

Case Example Three—Mike, Nine-Year-Old Boy

Mike was referred by parents for behavior problems at school. He was suspended for an anger outburst.

Presenting Problems:

Chronic problems with impulse control, anger behavior with peers, and verbal and physical aggression at school.

Treatment Goals:

1. Reduce anger behavior at school and teach Mike appropriate expression of anger.
2. Improve self concept.
3. Improve Mike's relationship with his parents and sister.

Theories	Techniques
1) Cognitive-Behavioral	• Anger management skill training for impulse control and appropriate outlets for aggression.
	• Token economy with daily school behavior report card and daily reinforcers for improvements.

	• Positive reinforcement of play in session after Mike first worked on behavior problem treatment.
	• Social skills training through school counselor.
2) Systems	• Family therapy to deal with father-son conflicts and sibling conflict with older sister.
3) Client-centered	• Self-concept building using supportive play therapy and therapeutic games in which Mike could experience success, take risks, and cope with winning and losing.

These three case examples illustrate the importance of a theoretical basis for treatment techniques.

PRACTICAL EXERCISE

1. Recall a recent case. What theoretical model(s) did you use?

- How were your techniques consistent with your theory?

- How effective was your treatment for this child?

- How comfortable were you in using this theoretical orientation?

  What areas of study do you need to help you provide "the necessary and sufficient conditions for change" for your client(s)?

2. Use this model to conduct a treatment plan with one of your clients.
   - Description of client:

   - Presenting Problems:

   - Treatment Goal(s):

Theories	Techniques

• Summary:

CHILDQUOTE

On Birth Control

Five-year-old Timmy was receiving a kindergarten screening by a colleague of mine. As usual, the examiner was asking basic get-acquainted questions prior to beginning formal testing. Questions included: How old are you? When is your birthday? Do you have any brothers or sisters? Timmy answered these questions, giving the names of his brother and baby sister. Timmy initiated further conversation by declaring, "We aren't going to have any more babies." The examiner asked, "Oh, why is that?" Timmy answered, "Because my Mommy had her boobs tied."

Part II

Tools of the Trade

BASIC PLAY THERAPY MATERIALS

Descriptions and Uses

If play is the language of children and toys are their words, what materials does a play therapist need to provide for children?

Most of my child therapy sessions have been conducted in an ordinary 12' × 15' office that contains a desk, chairs, sofa, cabinet, and child's table. The play therapy materials are in a cabinet or container easily accessible to children. A play therapy room specifically equipped for children is also available. It is good to have a special room, but you can be an effective play therapist using a regular office.

Here are the basic play materials I use and recommend:

TOYS

Miniature Dollhouse with Furniture and Doll Families

The house should be sturdy, easily accessible to children, and have furniture the children can arrange. I have several doll families for children to choose from in selecting "who lives in your house."

The house is a vehicle by which the child can express his view of family life. In a child's play with a house, I look for these themes:

- Who does she include in the house?
- With what role does she identify? Examples: a controlling or helpless role.
- Who does she exclude?
- Aggression: To whom and by whom?
- Nurturing: From whom or for whom?
- Safety: Are children secure or frightened?
- Are the activities typical family activities such as eating, sleeping, playing, working, or are they chaotic and destructive?

You can purchase a dollhouse from a toy store or a play therapy supply company. I particularly like a house contained in a wooden suitcase. When opened, there is a houseful of wooden furniture and several doll families; when not in use, the house is easily stored.

Clay

I recommend modeling clay that doesn't dry out. It can be purchased from an arts and crafts store.

Choose bright colors, earth tones, and somber shades. This encourages the child to express himself using colors that suit him today.

Keep the clay in a plastic container. Provide a flat tray for the child to "make something you like" or suggest, "I would like you to build something with the clay and tell me a story about it. I will help you if you like."

Themes frequently observed in play with clay:

- Expressive versus inhibited.
- Creative versus concrete.
- Positive versus negative.
- Controlled aggression versus destructive aggression.
- Fears versus safety.

Clay provides sensory stimulation of touch and encourages the child to express herself. Clay is formless and allows the youngster to project her own meaning onto the project. Most children respond easily and enthusiastically to play with clay. For the reluctant, or hesitant, child I usually offer to make something with the clay also. I am not a good artist, but that doesn't matter to the child. I often ask, "What is your favorite kind of animal?" When the child tells me, I make a clay replica. The child usually identifies with the animal, includes it in his play, and may make his own animals.

I note how much the child is able to affiliate with me. Does he engage in joint play?

Does he prefer to have me only as an observer? I introduce a story theme, see if the child picks it up and includes it in his activity. Children learn well with animated stories and I encourage them.

Toy Animals

I provide an assortment of types including wild animals, farm animals, pet animals, and dinosaurs that are two to three inches tall. The animals should be generic (not the latest movie or television monsters) so that the child can project onto the animal the features he chooses.

It is easy for children to identify with particular animals. They use the animal(s) to express major concerns such as fears, sadness, aggression, desires, nurturing, jealousy, love. I often use clay and animals together in play activity and in storytelling. (See Chapter Six for use of toys in mutual storytelling.)

Toy People

An assortment of plastic doll families, soldiers, police, firemen, and medical personnel two to five inches in height are useful. Doll families should include babies, children, parents and grandparents.

Toy people are used in play with the dollhouse, sand tray, and with clay. The toy people are kept in a collection so the child can choose the type of characters she wants for the day's session. I let the child choose which characters to begin with. I usually introduce additional people during the session to initiate themes related to treatment goals. Example: A child is in treatment due to problems with peers. If the child is playing only with the baby and parent dolls, I usually introduce peers in play to focus on the child's perception of peer relations.

Drawing Materials: Paper, Colored Markers, Crayons, Water Colors

Children's drawings are used for both diagnostic and treatment purposes.

For diagnosis, I recommend the House-Tree-Person drawing test (HTP) and the Kinetic Family Drawing test (KFD). For the HTP, I give these instructions, "I would like you to draw three pictures for me. On the first page, draw a house, any kind of house you want. On the second page, draw a tree. On the third page, draw a person and be sure to draw all of the person."

For the KFD, the instructions are, "I want you to draw a picture of your family for me. Put yourself in the picture and include whoever you want to be in your family drawing. Have every person doing some activity."

After the pictures are drawn, I ask the child to tell a short story about each one and I write down the story. The child's story usually adds significant diagnostic information.

I use these standard questions for HTP stories:

For the house drawing:

- Whose house this is?
- Where is it?
- Who lives in it?
- What is happening there?
- What will happen next?
- What do you like about that house?
- What do you not like about it?

For the tree drawing:

- What kind of tree did you draw?
- Where is that tree (location)?
- How old is it?
- Is it alive or dead?
- What will happen to that tree?

For the person drawing:

- Tell me a story about that person. Who is it?

- How old is that person?
- What is that person doing? Thinking? Feeling?
- What happened before this picture and what happens after the picture?
- What do you like the best?
- What do you like the least?

For the family drawing, I ask the child, "Tell me who everyone is. What is each person doing?" The people included and excluded are noted. Where the child positions himself in relation to family members, and what kind of activity the child reports, gives significant data regarding his perception of his family.

Drawings can be repeated during treatment to note whether the same themes still persist, and whether there has been improvement. Drawings are a basic therapeutic tool with most children. Children who have poor fine motor skills may not be responsive to drawing. For them, I use other toys, such as clay, people, and animals.

I encourage children to bring me drawings they made from school or home. In therapy sessions, free drawings are sometimes used. The child draws "anything you would like to draw for me today." Free drawings are designed to get the child to express herself.

I also use directed drawings. Examples are: For expression of emotions; "I want you to draw me several pictures: A time you were happy. A time you were mad. A time you were sad. A time you were afraid."

For understanding events in a child's history, ask the child to draw a picture of "When you were little, when you lived with (grandparents, foster parents, mother and father), what you like to do/what you wish to do."

Sand Tray

A sand tray can be made with a plastic storage box and sand from a building supply store. I use a tray approximately 48 inches long, 22 inches wide, and 8 inches deep. The tray should have a lid so it can be covered when not in use. I provide toy animals, people, and various vehicles.

Sand play provides children the sense of touch that most respond to with excitement. Typical themes in their play include battle scenes, race scenes, road building, castle building, and farm scenes. Unstructured sand play is enjoyable to most children ages three to nine years.

I observe the child's themes in free play, become involved as she invites me, and become more active by introducing themes related to treatment goals. Examples: In aggressive play with cars crashing, I may introduce aggression control themes such as building safety barriers or bringing in emergency vehicles or police to provide help and protection. With wild animals attacking other animals in child's play themes, I may add control, nurturing and protection themes by building a pen for the aggressive animal and providing food and water in the pen. The other animals may have a safe place with a fence and an "adult" protector.

Building Materials: Wooden Blocks, *Legos*, *Lincoln Logs*, *Tinker Toys*

Building blocks can be used in many ways. They are particularly helpful when children are in the Win and Win-Win stages of play (see Chapter Three). Win level is when the child plays alone and wants the therapist to be an interested observer, not an active participant. Win-Win level is when the child wants the therapist involved in joint activity in which both are winners.

Children use blocks to build houses, castles, towers, forts and towns. Blocks are neutral, so children can create their own world. Children can practice making, building, reproducing in a safe setting (absent criticism or demands) with a caring adult. At the end of a session of building, most children are eager to show their parents or caregivers what they have created.

I usually participate in block-building activities. Examples are: With a child whose parents are divorced, I may introduce the idea of building two houses, "Mommy's house" and "Daddy's house." If the child builds a castle that keeps falling down or gets knocked down, I reinforce the child's efforts at rebuilding. I may assist him in building, but always let the child finish the task so he can have the satisfaction of "I did it!"

Vehicles: Toy Cars, Trucks, Airplanes, Emergency and Construction Vehicles, and Space Ships

Toy vehicles are used in play with block building, clay, the sand tray, the dollhouse and storytelling. Children use vehicles to express fears, sadness, aggression, exploration, sense of control, giving and receiving help.

Police cars, fire trucks, and ambulances represent different things to children based on their experiences. I notice whether the child views police vehicles as helpers or threats. Are emergency vehicles available to help? I often introduce these vehicles to see how a child responds. I also use them to communicate to a child that I am available to help.

Dolls and Stuffed Animals

These are available for comfort and security. Children ages two to four particularly respond to using dolls and animals in play therapy. Children use them to "play out" their interests and concerns.

Puppets

Animal and people hand puppets are valuable in play therapy. I provide puppets of aggressive, neutral, and helpless characters. I note which puppets the child selects and how he uses certain puppets to express his concerns.

I often ask a child if he would like to put on a puppet show. Some children readily perform with me as an audience. Or I may perform with the child as audience or the child and I may do a show together. I always ask the child to tell me, "What is the moral of the story? What does it teach us?" If the child does not respond, I state a lesson or moral. Children like to recreate a puppet show for their parents or care-givers toward the end of a session.

Puppet play typically begins with the child and therapist exploring different puppets and interacting together. Examples: lion and elephant puppets growl-ing and fighting; mother sheep and lamb puppets seek-ing each other; dog and bear puppets exploring friend-ship; a wise owl puppet inviting another puppet to "Explore my forest." After such puppet play, the child is encouraged to act out a puppet story. I introduce themes related to the child's treatment needs in my puppet play with the child.

I have found animal puppets to be more effective than people puppets with most children. It is easier for a child to project his concerns onto an animal.

Telephones

Toy phones are useful with younger children. A pre-school child uses a play telephone in pretend play to talk with a parent or other caregiver. I use a phone to initiate a conversation topic with a child.

Examples:

Therapist: "Ring, ring, ring. Hello. Yes, he's here. Billy, it's your Mommy. She wants to talk with you."

Therapist: "Ring, ring, ring. Hello, Billy. This is Dr. Price. What are you doing?

Are you happy or sad today? Can I come over and help you? Okay. I'll be right over. Goodbye."

Toy Guns/Outlets for Aggression

The use of toy guns in the playroom is controversial. Some therapists view it as encouraging children to express aggression. A differing view is that the use of toy guns provides an outlet for this natural expression of aggressive impulses and that play with toy guns does not generalize to more aggression outside the playroom.

I have a toy gun available in the play cabinet. I do not encourage its use, but children use all kinds of objects as toy weapons in play therapy, including toy hammers, crayons, pool sticks, wands, and fingers. If guns are used in the therapy room, they must look like toys, not be replicas of an adult weapon. Use of guns and weapons that identify with a violent movie or comic character is strongly discouraged.

I like to provide outlets for anger and aggressive impulses. I have a cobbler's bench pounding block and hammer in the toy cabinet. Children use it often. An example is the child who comes into the office with lots of anger and begins the session with a high activity level and aggressive play. I may offer the child the pounding block as an outlet. The child may pound on the block for five to ten minutes, then be ready for more productive therapy time. Inflatable punching dolls can be useful for aggression outlets as well.

What we are looking for are appropriate outlets for aggression—ones the child uses to let go of anger. We do not want an activity that encourages or increases aggressive impulses. Example: If a punching bag becomes a stimulant to a child that increases aggressive play, I recommend stopping the activity. If the child hits the bag a few times and them becomes calmer, it has been a useful tool. I recommend that the therapist observe each particular child's mood and behavior to assess how much to use such aggression outlets as a punching bag, pounding block, toy gun, ball darts, or outdoor physical activities.

Tape Recorder

Audio tapes are particularly useful with storytelling. Most children love to hear themselves on tape. They can express their thoughts or tell a story about what they have made or done. I use the tape recorder to interview a child and in mutual storytelling. Often, children want to have their parents hear the playback of a recorded story. Chapter 6 on Storytelling describes the use of a tape recorder in greater detail.

Play Doctor's Kit

Children use the kit for role playing the powerful part of doctor and the needy position of the patient. Play with a stuffed animal, doll or puppet, and doctor's kit provides a means for the child to practice helping and being helped.

Wonder Toys

The playroom should stimulate the child's sense of wonder, awe, and beauty. I provide "wonder" toys such as a kaleidoscope and a space tube with floating stars, moons and snowflakes. My office is decorated with nature scenes of mountains, forests, lakes, and waterfalls. Cultivating a love of beauty and wonder is therapeutic.

GAMES

Which board games are useful in play therapy? A child's choice of a game and how she uses it suggests her developmental level of Win, Win/Win, Chance or Skill as described in Chapter 3.

Chance Games

These are games that involve dice, spinners, and cards. The element of chance is a major portion of the game. Such games require less ego risk for the child.

As the therapist, I also manipulate the chance of the child's winning or losing. The games are to meet the child's needs for relating to the therapist, for mastery of tasks, and for learning to accept victories and losses.

Examples:

Candyland
Sorry
Yahtzee
Card games such as *Animal Rummy* and *Uno*

Skill Games

Such games are for children with the ego strength to take the risk of expressing their abilities with the result of success or loss. Children with less ego strength or high control needs tend to manipulate skill games and chance games through changing the rules or cheating. The game a child chooses, how she plays, and her emotional reactions are all significant in understanding her developmental level, emotional state, and type of therapeutic intervention needed.

Examples:

Connect Four, Checkers, Chess, miniature pool games or *Carrom* games, target or sports games such as miniature bowling or basketball.

Therapeutic Games

Richard Gardner's *Thinking, Feeling, Doing* (1973) game is a board game using cards that asks players to respond to questions about thoughts, feelings, and actions.

Some cards ask for humorous responses, others for serious responses. The game uses chips as rewards for answering the questions. The therapist can arrange the topic cards beforehand, based on the needs of the child and the topics to include. Children reluctant to talk about personal matters will often respond to the structure of a game. The *Ungame* (1989) is another therapeutic game. These can be purchased at some bookstores and from play therapy companies.

Outdoor Games

Children who are reluctant, or inhibited, in expressing themselves in the office, may respond when we do outdoor activities. Some children will "talk on the go" but not when sitting down. Taking a walk, playing catch or swinging in a nearby park can be helpful. Caution: When taking a child out of the office, be certain the parent knows where you are going and that he or she approves. Conduct the activity in a public setting where you can be observed.

During a walk or outdoor game, I talk to the child about his treatment issues and encourage the child to talk about his concerns.

Children will not remember much of your verbal wisdom, but they will long remember what you did together. Adolescent patients whom I treated five or more years ago invariably remember the play activities and games they did in therapy as children.

For my list of most important toys see Appendix 3.

SYMBOLS THAT TOYS REPRESENT FOR CHILDREN

Children use toys as symbols to express their concerns, needs, thoughts, and feelings. Just as words have different meanings based on a person's perception, understanding, experience, and the setting in which the words are used, so toys take on different meanings based on the child's perception, experience and situation. In play therapy, the therapist works to understand the symbols that particular toys represent to the child.

Symbols for Aggression

Typical toys are large animals such as lions, elephants, dinosaurs, and monsters. Race cars, authority figures, and toy guns are other aggression symbols. The child may use these to express external aggression threats from others and/or his own aggressive impulses.

Symbols for Danger or Threat

Children use storms, crashes, authority figures, and large animals. The same toy may be used by a child to be a symbol of danger and fear or as a symbol of power for a child. A child may identify with a toy lion that attacks other animals and people, or use the lion as a symbol of outside danger threatening his smaller animal or person.

Symbols for Nurturing

Toys and activities include bedtime in doll play with children being tucked in bed, giving "food" and "water" in dollhouse play or with clay, feeding animals, or using a doctor's kit to "fix" an injured doll or animal.

Symbols for Safety and Protection

Typical symbols are building a house or cave for people or animals. I often help a child build a fence, a wall, or a home to help protect the animal or person the child has identified. The fence or pen may be a symbol of limit-setting for an out-of-control animal.

Marty (Chapter One) used an imaginary jail in which to put "monsters" so he could feel safe and protected.

Symbols for Dependence, Helplessness, and Weakness

Baby people and animals, sick or hurt, are common symbols for helplessness. In doll play, children often act out their sense of weakness, dependence, and need to be cared for.

Symbols for Autonomy, Independence, and Freedom

Children use autonomy words such as "Mine," "No," "Let me do it," "I did it myself!" They also use toys and activities to express autonomy. The story that uses smaller horses or other animals to go away from the bigger animals may be expressing autonomy. When a child builds a block tower, house, or building, she may be using the building as a symbol of her autonomy.

Toy vehicles are often used as a symbol for independence. The child who takes a car or airplane and goes on a trip likely is expressing a sense of independence and freedom.

Symbols for Power and Mastery

Gaining power to control and choose is a strong need for children. I introduce and encourage play themes that empower the child to handle situations and to obtain mastery over a task. I use attention and praise to reinforce the mastery of a situation or the completion of a task.

Examples are a child's drawings, clay or sand creations, building with blocks or *Legos*. Mastery is expressed with sayings like "Mommy, look, at what I made." By giving the child limited choices of activities such as, "Today, do you want to play with the clay and animals or the puppets?" the child has some control over this part of his life at a level he can handle.

Children often use the dollhouse, the building they have made, the race or battle scene, the puppet show, or the clay creation to gain control over a situation.

Toy play can provide a safe setting for a child to practice problem solving , self control and mastery over difficult problems.

Case Example:

Jill was a five-year old girl who had pinched and shaken her two-month-old infant brother repeatedly because of sibling jealously. Her parents brought her to me in fear and frustration because they had not been able to stop this behavior. At my recommendation, Jill stayed with other family members for three days.

In the first session, Jill used the dollhouse to represent her home and how she had "messed with my baby brother." She was fully aware why she had come to see me. Jill practiced with the dolls how the sister gained control over her anger impulses. She demonstrated this in front of her parents. Jill went home and exhibited self control the next week The parents reported no more serious aggressive behavior toward her infant brother the entire week after this play therapy session.

The toys described in this chapter are useful in helping a child play out her story and receive therapeutic intervention.

Chapter 6 is devoted to mutual storytelling, a major tool of play therapy.

PRACTICAL EXERCISE

1. Take an inventory of your play therapy material.

2. Rate your toy collection: Incomplete _____
   Complete _____
   If incomplete, what toys do you want to add?

3. Comfort and skill levels.
   a) With which toys/games are you the most comfortable?

   Least comfortable?

   b) With which toys or games do you consider yourself the most skilled?

   With which least skilled?

   c) Plans for improvement:

CHILDQUOTE

On Child's Understanding

Six-year-old Brenda states that she had heard her Mom and Dad discussing an adult subject. When she asked her Mom a question, her mother responded with, "You're too young; you wouldn't understand."

Brenda declared to me, "They don't know that I know; I'm a lot smarter than I look."

Child's Insight

Six-year-old Marilyn referring to times she and her father had angry arguments: "Parents get mad at you sometimes, but they still love you."

6

THERAPEUTIC STORYTELLING

Mutual Storytelling Technique and Different Variations

Storytelling is an excellent way to communicate with children. Most children love stories.

"Mommy, will you read me a story?"

"Daddy, tell me a story about when . . . ."

Children become fascinated with the characters and events in a story and often identify with particular characters. Stories help children learn sequence: beginning, middle, and end. Stories are easier to remember than conversation, for they capture the imagination through creative use of fantasy.

Great religious and moral literature rely heavily on use of stories. The Bible is full of stories. *Aesop's Fables* are a collection of short stories with a moral.

Therapeutic storytelling is a specialized use of stories to help the child express her problems, concerns, hopes, and fears and is an effective means for the therapist to communicate understanding and intervention. I have found it to be a major component of play therapy.

GARDNER'S MUTUAL STORYTELLING TECHNIQUE

I have profited greatly from Richard Gardner's contribution to therapeutic storytelling. His technique is one in which the therapist uses a child's self-created stories therapeutically. The child tells a story and the therapist interprets its meaning. Then the therapist tells a story that includes the same characters in a similar setting, but introduces healthier adaptations and resolutions of the conflicts than have been expressed by the child.

Gardner states that by speaking in a child's own language, there is a greater chance that the message will be heard and incorporated into the child's psychic structure. Resistance is reduced. Direct, anxiety-producing confrontations, similar to the child's experiences with parents and teachers, are avoided.

Gardner uses audio and video recorders in his storytelling. These allow children the opportunity to listen to or watch their recorded stories.

A thorough presentation of Gardner's storytelling technique is found in his book *Therapeutic Communication with Children—The Mutual Storytelling Technique* by Richard A. Gardner (1971).

Gardner also describes his technique in *Hand-*

book of Play Therapy edited by Schaefer and O'Connor, pp. 356–357:

"I begin by asking the child if he or she would like to be guest of honor on a make-believe television program on which stories are told. If the child agrees—and few decline the honor—the recorder is turned on and I begin: 'Good morning boys and girls, ladies and gentlemen. I'm happy to welcome you once again to Dr. Gardner's 'Make-up-a-Story Television Program.' On this program, we invite children to see how good they are at making up stories. It's against the rules to tell any stories about anything that really happened to you or anyone you know. The story cannot be about anything you've seen on television, heard on the radio, or read in books. Naturally, the more adventure or excitement the story has, the more fun it will be to watch on television afterward. After you finish your story, you tell us the moral or lesson of your story. And everyone knows that every good story has a lesson or moral.' Then, Dr. Gardner will make up a story and he'll tell the lesson or moral of his story.

"And now, I'm very happy to tell you that we have a new boy (girl) who is with us for the first time today. Can you tell us your name, young man (lady)?"

The child is asked easy-to-answer questions such as age, address, school, grade, and teacher which reduce any anxiety related to making up a story. Gardner then says,

> "Now that we've heard a few things about you, we're all interested in hearing the story you have for us today. You're on the air."

The child then begins his story. During the story, Gardner writes notes to help him analyze the child's story and prepare for his own story. When the child finishes, Gardner asks for the lesson or moral.

Following the child's story, Gardner then creates a story of his own using the same characters in the child's story in a similar setting. His goal is to determine the inapproprate or maladaptive themes in the child's stories and to introduce "healthier modes of adaptation and healthier methods of resolution than those revealed in the child's story." After completing the story, Gardner asks the child to try to figure out the lesson or moral of the therapist's story to help determine if his message has been understood. If the child is not successful in figuring out the moral, Gardner then presents it.

After the therapist's story, he generally tries to engage the child in a discussion of its meaning based on the child's ability to gain insight and/or refer to self. Gardner does not press for insights because "I believe that the important therapeutic element is to get across a principle—and that this principle, per se, can contribute significantly to therapeutic change and alteration of behavior."

MY USE OF MUTUAL STORYTELLING TECHNIQUE

I use a similar approach to Gardner's technique, but put less emphasis on interpretation of the story. The following is a transcript of Sandra's first mutual story telling time.

Case Example One—Sandra, Five-Year-Old Girl

Sandra was a five-year-old girl in foster care who, along with her three-year-old brother, was in need of an adoptive home. Her biological mother had emotional problems and tried unsuccessfully to care for Sandra on two separate occasions prior to relinquishing parental rights.

Dr. Price:	"Good morning, boys and girls. Welcome to Dr. Price's story-telling time. Today my special guest is Sandra. Would you say hello to the boys and girls?"
Sandra:	"Hello."
Dr. Price:	"How old are you?"
Sandra:	"Five and a half."
Dr. Price:	"Sandra goes to afternoon kindergarten. Who is your teacher?"
Sandra:	"Miss Becky."
Dr. Price:	"What do you like to do in kindergarten?"
Sandra:	"I like to color pictures."

Dr. Price:	"Sandra, you're very good at coloring. You have drawn me a pretty picture of flowers. This is the third time that Sandra has been to see me. She likes to draw and she likes to play with the dollhouse.

Today boys and girls, Sandra is going to tell you a story. It's one she has made up all by herself. It isn't from a book or television show. It's one of the many stories she has in her head. When she's finished with the story, Sandra will tell us the moral: That's what the story teaches us.

Sandra, do you have a story to tell the boys and girls?" |
Sandra:	"Yes, about a family."
Dr. Price:	"Okay. So when she's ready, h-e-r-e-'s S-a-n-d-r-a!"
Sandra:	"Once upon a time, there was a family, two kids, a Mommy and there was a Daddy and another girl came. They were poor people. They did not have anything to eat. No water, no food, no breakfast, a little bit of clothes; that's all. I want to hear my voice."
Dr. Price:	"Can you tell us what that story teaches us?"
Sandra:	"Teaches us how poor people do without any food or water."

I interpreted Sandra's story to be about her needs for nurturing and for a family.

My followup story:

Dr. Price: "Once upon a time there was a family, a Mommy and Daddy and kids that were very poor. They didn't have food; just a few clothes. They got cold and hungry and didn't have much to drink (I'm referring to the neglect she had experienced prior to foster care). Then some people came and gave the kids some food and water (I'm referring to the present foster home where Sandra was receiving excellent care). And they got something to eat and drink. But you know what? Even when they had lots of clothes and food, they still got scared 'cause they were afraid they wouldn't have food again (I'm referring to Sandra's insecurity about who would be there for her). And it took them a long time to get used to having food and clothes and water. The end. The story teaches:

Take care of the children so they won't be scared and they will have plenty to eat and drink."

Sandra was eager to use storytelling. Her short story was Sandra's way of expressing her history of neglect, her fears and insecurity related to neglect and her strong need for nurturing.

My story was designed to express recognition of her pain related to past neglect and separation from her biological mother, understanding of her current situation in foster care and her desire for a new family.

VARIATIONS OF MUTUAL STORYTELLING

I use several variations of mutual storytelling including: I'll Tell You a Story, Continuous Story, Fill in the Blank Story. The common theme in all is to provide an encouraging means for children to express themselves—their joy, sadness, pain, anger, fear, hope, desire. It also provides me an excellent way to communicate understanding and intervention with a story.

Variation One: "I'll Tell You a Story"

An example is Sandra's mutual storytelling. Sandra was eager to find a new family. She was very sociable and verbal about her desires. She had recently had a failed adoption placement. The prospective adoptive family took her home on a Friday with the stated intention of being Sandra's new Mom and Dad. But on Monday, they called the adoptive agency stating they had changed their minds. This was in addition to two failed placements with her biological mother.

In a subsequent therapy session, I wanted to deal

with Sandra's history of separation and loss and with the recent rejection by adoptive parents. I used this story:

Dr. Price: "Hello, boys and girls. Welcome to Storytelling Time. Sandra, would you say hello to the boys and girls?"

Sandra: "Hello."

Dr. Price: "Sandra and I have been playing with clay and animals. Today, I have a story. When I finish my story, Sandra can tell her own story if she wants to. My story today is about little goat. Goat was looking for a home. He used to have a home where he lived on a mountain, but the mountain got torn down. He started looking for a new home. The first mountain he found was too tall and he fell off and got hurt, so he didn't stay there. The next time, he went and found a little hill, but he didn't like it much because it wasn't good for climbing, and goats need a place to climb. Then he found some other animals—some giraffes, sheep, and zebras. They became his friends and they said, 'Go with us.' His friends helped him look for a home. They looked and looked and they found a place that had water to drink from the river, grass to eat, and trees to get under when it was hot, and guess what? It was a nice mountain, the right size and he got to climb a mountain and look, because goats like to climb mountains. He said, 'I like this place. This will be my home.' The end. It's a story about how the goat finally found his home."

In this story, I addressed Sandra's eagerness for a home. The goat's experience represented that the search was long. I wanted to convey the message that the multiple placements were not Sandra's fault, thus the search included a "too tall" and a "too small" mountain. The animal friends represented adults other than birth family who cared for her now and were looking for a placement for Sandra and her little brother.

The search ends when Goat finds a home that meets his needs for nurturing, safety and exploration as represented by the stream, food and the "right size" mountain.

After my story, Sandra was ready to tell hers. Some children as sociable and verbal as she want to tell their own story. Others do not. I do discuss the issues in my story at the level the child is ready to accept, and I speak in a direct manner.

Here's Sandra's succinct but powerful story that followed mine:

Dr. Price: "Now Sandra's going to tell her story. Nobody knows what it is, only Sandra, because it's her story. Here it is."

Sandra: "Once upon a time when I was a little bitty baby, I growed in my Mommy's tummy. And a lady used to babysit me. So my Mommy took me to Mary's (her present foster mother). And I miss my Mommy very much. Have to find me another Mommy. The end. I want to hear my voice."

I use this variation when I want to present a theme related to the child's situation.

When I do not have the rapport that I had with Sandra, this is a typical way I begin.

Dr. Price: "I'd like to tell you a story today. At the end, I will give the story a moral: that's what the story teaches. Do you want the story to be about people or animals? (If the answer is a person) Big or little people? Boy or girl, man or woman? (If the choice is an animal) What kind of animal do you want?"

I then tell a story that parallels an important area of the child's life. If this is an early play therapy session, I base my story on background information and the presenting problems told me by the parents. The child's response to my story lets me know if I'm on track or whether I am too direct. I adjust the future stories based on the child's response.

I ask, "Do you have a story for me?" This is optional for the child. Children who are less verbal than Sandra or who are more inhibited tend not to tell their own story, but will act out their concerns through play, often with clay and animals.

Other variations are used to encourage children to participate in therapeutic stories.

Variation Two: Continuous Story

I use this type introduction:

Dr. Price: "Good afternoon, boys and girls. Today is (give date) and my special guest is Amy. Would you say hello to the boys and girls? Today, Amy and I are going to tell a story together. I will begin the story and come to a stopping point; then Amy will pick up the story until she comes to a stopping point. We will do this at least twice until we are ready to end the story. At the end, Amy will tell the moral of our story, what it teaches us; then I will also give the story a moral. Amy, do you want our story today to be about people or animals?"

I begin with a story that relates to the child's circumstances and needs—such as separation fears, sadness, divorce or death in the family, family problems. I bring the story to a dilemma, stop and ask the child to continue the story. The child responds to the dilemma, then continues the story using her own themes. The child comes to a decisive point, stops and has me respond to the dilemma. We repeat this process one or more times.

By presenting a key issue that applies to the

child's situation I see how the child reacts. I can also determine how ready the child is to deal with that situation, what coping resources and problem-solving skills she uses, and hear the concerns that the child expresses in her portions of the continuous story.

Example: Rhonda was a ten-year-old girl who was referred to me for treatment of severe headaches that resulted in her missing school several days each week for more than a month. Extensive medical tests had not revealed any organic cause of her headaches. Rhonda's parents were distressed that they had been unable to find a cause or an effective treatment for her headaches.

My treatment involved behavioral therapy, parent consultation, and individual play therapy. Storytelling was used with this bright girl to facilitate verbal expression of her concerns at a level she was willing to share.

In this continuous story, Rhonda introduces problems and resolutions; she uses a divorce theme, although her parents had never been divorced and reported no marital problems. The content was not an accurate description of her family, as far as I knew, but Rhonda used it as a means to express her anger and release.

Dr. Price: "Once upon a time, there was a child who loved to learn and have fun and exercise, climb mountains, swim, and read. But something happened, a problem came that took away the enjoyment. (I began my story with a child

somewhat similar to Rhonda. I wanted
to hear what she would do with such a
theme.) And the problem was . . . ."

Rhonda: "The parents got divorced. Okay. She
was really mad 'cause she heard her parents fighting but she didn't really think
it was that bad. And when they told her
that, she went to her room and started
crying. Then she decided she would
never talk to her parents again, and she
didn't want to live with any of them because she was so mad."

Dr. Price: "It was shocking to know that the arguments had really gotten this bad. Besides
being scared, she was mad and said,
'Why did you do this?' She was so mad.
She kept her mad for a pretty long time.
Then, she went from being mad to sad.
She couldn't understand why this happened. She started moping. Sometimes
she would be mad, sometimes sad. And
this lasted for . . . ."

Rhonda: "Over a month. And finally she was being really mean to her friends and she
was drifting away from all her friends.
She just kept getting more and more to
herself. (Rhonda described her own
withdrawal and self-absorption due to
her psychosomatic pain.) Finally, her
parents made her go to a special doctor
for kids whose parents are divorced.
(Rhonda accepts the idea of seeing a psy-

chologist rather than another medical specialist.) And they started talking; she told him all about her life and . . . ."

Dr. Price: "That seemed to help some although it was kinda hard to do. But once she did it and talked to other kids, some of the mad and hurt came out. She found that some of her strength started to come back so that . . . ."

Rhonda: "She was nice again. And she could finally understand that it was for the best and if her parents didn't get divorced, they would always be mad and yelling at each other. It wouldn't be a happy life . . . ."

Dr. Price: "As painful as it was, there was some good because they both still loved her and she would still get to be with them. It was just hard getting used to the home being different. And at the end . . . ."

Rhonda: "She got used to it. And both her parents got married. And she wasn't very happy about that. She talked to her Mom and they decided that she could stay with both her parents, with one parent one week and the other parent the next week. And she finally said okay. She got used to it and started a school for kids whose parents are divorced . . . ."

Dr. Price: "And that is the story of how the girl learned to cope with something as hard as divorce." (My conclusion was to make the comparison that Rhonda and her family were going through a very difficult time, as difficult as if her parents really did get a divorce.) "Do you want to give the story a moral?"

Rhonda: "Bad things happen . . . ."

Dr. Price: "And when you're hurting because something happens, it's okay to reach out for help."

Two significant stressors appeared to be the main contributors to Rhonda's chronic headaches and present depressed mood. First, the family moved from out-of-state the previous year. Rhonda missed her old friends and had difficulty in making new friends. She didn't adjust well to the change of moving. Second, Rhonda's mother began working outside the home for the first time in her daughter's life.

Rhonda reacted by becoming sick with headaches, staying home from school often, and necessitating more involvement from both her parents. She withdrew into her world of books and homework assignments, repressed her anger, and became a miserable young girl.

I used the Continuous Story technique in an effort to help Rhonda express her pain. This seemed more appropriate than just focusing on headache management, which had become her family's major focus. She responded well, identifying her anger toward family changes, accepting the idea of professional help from a non-physician, and began to utilize her cognitive skills in problem solving.

Rhonda was able to use mutual storytelling along with behavior therapy of relaxation training and stress management. Within five sessions her headaches reduced significantly, her depression lifted and she returned to school and friendship building.

See Chapter Seven, page 129 in which Rhonda's case is an example of treating a child with a diagnosis of Adjustment Disorder with Depressed Mood.

Variation Three: Fill-in-the-Blanks Story

I have found this approach particularly useful with younger children ages five through nine, with children reluctant to engage in anything other than a brief conversation, and with children who have difficulty using fantasy in play.

Example: Zachary was a five-year-old boy with Attention Deficit Hyperactivity Disorder and Anxiety Adjustment Disorder. He recently moved into a blended family that included his father, stepmother, an eight-year-old half sister, a ten-year-old half brother, and two teenage step brothers. Zachary was having significant behavior problems in kindergarten and daycare, along with being very demanding for attention at home.

The story theme fit Zachary and he responded well in giving short responses to my open-ended sentences.

Dr. Price: "Once upon a time, there was a little tiger named Tony. Sometimes he would run and play and have so much fun. And he would help. . . . "

Zachary: "Except he got mad 'cause he didn't want to go to the daycare center (Zachary identified one of the major problems he had daily)."

Dr. Price: "He didn't like it. He didn't want to go there. He got mad. Do you know what he did? He practiced like a big tiger. He tried to roar.

He went R-O-A-R! He was really mad. And he stayed mad until. . . . "

Zachary: "Next year."

Dr. Price: "Some of the other tigers at daycare didn't like him because he roared and he was so mad. But, another day he felt good and the other tigers liked to play with him. One special day, something happened. All of a sudden. . . . "

Zachary: "R-O-A-R said the teacher."

Dr. Price: "The teacher was roaring, too. Tony didn't know what to do. So he thought and thought. And here's what he did . . . ."

Zachary: "He was shy and then he stopped talk-ing."

Dr. Price: "He stopped talking and he started learning tiger language and tiger things. And he didn't get his name on the board much . . . ."

Zachary: "Only one letter."

Dr. Price: "Only one time. One day, Tony was sad. You know why? He couldn't find his mother." (I introduced the mother theme. His biological mother lived out of state and his stepmother and he were just forming an attachment.)

Dr. Price: "So here's what he did . . . ."

Zachary: "The mother was the teacher." (Zachary seemed to identify the current caregivers as his maternal figures.)

Dr. Price: "One day his Dad said, 'Tony, I'm going to take you out to teach you how to hunt for food like tigers do.'" (I introduced his father as an important caregiver and role model. Zachary had been separated from his father except for periodic visits for at least a year, but he was now heavily involved in Zachary's daily care.) "So they went to the forest and started hunting for food. And this is what happened . . . ."

Zachary: "You tell it."

Dr. Price: "They found some food and it tasted real good and Tony was happy. And they started to get some more food but couldn't find it . . . ."

Zachary: "So a bear came down and they killed it, so they got some more food."

Dr. Price: "And the Daddy tiger said, 'You are going to grow up and be a good helper. We'll go hunting for food again, but most

	of the time, I'll get it for you.' (I presented father as main provider.) So they went back to their home; it was in a cave." (Here I introduce anxiety related to a new home and a new family configuration.) "And the cave was dark and kinda scary. Tony didn't know what to do and . . . ."
Zachary:	"He ran (an accurate statement of his high activity level at home)."
Dr. Price:	"His dad said, 'Why are you running?' Tony said, 'Because it's dark in there and I'm scared. So Dad said, 'I'll put a light in the cave for you.' Tony went in and there were shadows on the wall. It was scary and . . . ."
Zachary:	"It was theirselves."
Dr. Price:	"Then he got used to it and he liked it. It was dry and cozy and had all kinds of places to play . . . ." (The present home was nurturing with clear limits.)
Zachary:	"The end."

Storytelling as Part of Play Activities

"Tell me a story about what you have made" is a frequent statement I use with a child during play therapy. Whether the activitiy is a drawing, clay and animals, puppets, dollhouse play, or sand tray, the child is encouraged to express himself with a story. I assume the role of an interested observer.

I listen to the child, and if needed, help the child articulate his story by asking questions and making suggestions. From the child's story, I usually move to roles of active involvement in the child's activity, introducing therapeutic themes, and begin discussion of the child's problems. Variations of the mutual storytelling technique are also used in connection with these play activities.

Case Example One—Charlie, Four-Year-Old Boy

Charlie was referred by his parents for severe behavior problems in day care. His parents were called frequently by day care workers due to Charlie's aggressive behavior of hitting other children and refusing to obey the teachers. He had been dismissed from another day care earlier in the year.

In the first session, while I was interviewing his mother, I gave Charlie clay and assorted plastic animals. He immediately became involved in play. Charlie's mother was perplexed and frustrated with her son. She described his history of behavior problems and concluded with, "I just don't know what the problem is. I don't know what to do with Charlie. We've tried everything we can."

Charlie's play theme was diagnostic. While his mother was talking, Charlie made a zoo with several animals. He identified with the lion and acted out a brief story. The lion attacked other animals, the zoo keeper couldn't control him, and the lion ran away from the zoo. I became involved in Charlie's story. I built a cave with a fence around it for the lion. Charlie helped me put the lion in the cave and it did not run away again.

In this short play session, Charlie presented his situation to his mother and me: He was the lion that was out of control and needed limits. My treatment goals seemed clear. I would focus on a behavior management program for daycare and home, aggression and its control with Charlie, regular parent consultation regarding the need for clear rules and routine in his life, and social skills training on taking turns and group participation for this only child.

Case Example Two—Jacob, Eleven-Year-Old Boy

I treated Jacob for a severe case of generalized anxiety with obsessive fears and worries. His fears included "I'm scared of growing up, becoming an adult, and being on my own." He was afraid of separation from his parents, their dying, and of storms. Jacob had had several months of cognitive behavior treatment. His anxiety, which had been at eight to nine on a scale of one to ten, had reduced to a four.

Drawings and storytelling were used to assess Jacob's fear of the future and his present coping ability. Jacob's favorite drawings were of airplanes. When I asked him to draw a picture of his choice, he drew an "F-16 fighter-bomber." Jacob's drawing was detailed and neat. The plane was camouflaged. He responded to the continuous story technique using his drawing as the topic. Jacob included himself and the therapist as pilots on a mission. In my portions of the story, I included themes of risks, facing dangers, practicing safety procedures and enjoying beautiful scenery as part of the mission. Jacob responded to my themes with his emphasis upon the therapist being his partner on flights, continuing the mission despite dangers and ending with his safe arrival.

Jacob's moral for his story was, "always do the best you can with what you have. I think it teaches us that the pilots handled it properly and did a good job."

Jacob's story expressed improved facing and coping with anxiety, his identification with the therapist as his helper and a manageable level of fear. Although anxieties were still present, the storytelling plus parent and Jacob's reports indicated that only periodic treatment was now needed.

A CHILD'S LIFE STORY

Telling her life story is a technique I have used with a child. I have the child dictate her story and I write it down. I have the child design her cover page. I suggest making a personal shield with pictures of "things that are important to you." I help the child organize her story by using topics such as: When I Was Little, Places I Lived, Caregivers, School, Happy Times, Sad Times, What I Have Learned, or What I Would Like Other Children to Know.

Case Example One—Deanna, Ten-Year-Old Girl

Deanna was in foster care and responded well to telling her life story. She had lived in two foster homes, her mother's parental rights were recently terminated, and Deanna was waiting for an adoptive home placement. This is what she dictated regarding "What I would like other kids to know."

"That I'm very smart." Deanna was behind in school when she was in the second grade and had worked hard to improve. Now in the fourth grade, she was reading at grade level and loved to read chapter books.

"I can be nice when I want to. I can do good in sports sometimes. And if I don't, I'm sorry." Deanna had a strong need for acceptance and approval from adults and peers.

"That it's not their fault if they have to go to foster care for some reason and if their parents wasn't able to take care of them, and they never lived with their parent any more. If they were going to be adopted, it'll be okay; at least they have a home."

Deanna was able to recall her childhood memories and describe disruptive and painful experiences when she lived with her biological mother and grandmother. She expressed her likes and dislikes and told about her foster care placements. She was working at making the best she could out of painful separation and loss experiences. Deanna's life story cover page was in bright colors with many hearts and balloon decorations.

Deanna kept a copy of her life story and gave me

a copy. We referred to this story several times in later sessions.

A Typical Outline for a Child's Life Story

I.   Childhood Memories
   • Some things I remember when I was little; when I was older.
   • Some places I lived.
II. What I Remember about School.
   • Some schools I attended
   • What I like and don't like about school.
III. Important People in My Life.
   • Adults
   • Friends
IV. Likes and dislikes
   • Some things I like.
   • Some things I don't like.
V.   My Life Now.
VI. Some Things I Have Learned.
VII. What I Want to Do and Be in the Future.
VIII. What I Would Like Other Kids and Adults to Know.

USE OF AUDIO AND VIDEO TAPES

I recommend using audio and video tapes with your clients. Most children respond well to the use of these tapes in play therapy. The use of an imaginary audience is a strong encourager. "I want to hear my story" is a common response from children. I keep a supply of audio tapes in my office. Each child labels his tape and keeps it in a cassette case readily available to him. Children often want their parents to hear their taped stories. Frequently parents will compliment their child with "that's a good story." From listening to the child's tapes parents can better understand their child's concerns and become more involved in therapy.

BIBLIOTHERAPY: READING THERAPEUTIC STORIES TO CHILDREN

I have favorite stories that I read to children in the four-to-eight-year range. The stories open up opportunities to talk with children about similar events in their lives.

Examples:

1. For a child who is grieving over the loss of a family member or friend:

   I'll Miss You, Mr. Hooper. This book is about Big Bird's sadness at the death of Mr. Hooper, remembering experiences with Mr. Hooper and his difficulty with the concept of death being permanent.

   I read this story to a four-year-old boy whose mother had recently died. It helped him express his sadness. Soon afterwards, he talked about missing his mother and said, "She died; she won't be coming back any more."

2. For a child coping with divorce:

    Dinosaur's Divorce. It presents the common grief reactions in coping with divorce, visitation, holidays and blended family. I have found it very useful.

3. For a child diagnosed with Attention Deficit Disorder.

    Shelley, The Hyperactive Turtle. This book helps the young child understand what Attention Deficit Disorder is and the treatment involved.

PRACTICAL EXERCISE

1. Use the Mutual Storytelling Technique with a child using an audio or video tape recorder. What was the child's theme?

    • What did the child state was the moral or lesson of her story?

    • What was your story and the moral?

    • How did the child react to your story?

- Did the storytelling time lead to the child being able to talk about his or her pain?
  Yes _____ No _____ Describe.

2. Use one of the Storytelling Variations described in this chapter.
   - What was the child's theme?

   - What did the child state as the moral?

   - What was your story and moral?

   - How did the child respond to your story?

     Did the storytelling time lead to the child being able to talk about his or her pain?
     Yes _____ No _____ Describe.

CHILDQUOTE

Empathy of Children

I was standing in the checkout line at the local garden center. In front of me was a frustrated mother and her two children, ages approximately seven and five years. The children were restless, climbing in and out of the bottom of the cart, which was loaded with various plants and flowers. The mother repeated for the fifth time, "Will you please be still?" The five-year-old son, in a move to demand attention, walked off and returned carrying a plant from a nearby cart.

Mother:	"Jason, where did you get that?"
Son:	"I don't know."
Mother:	"Now you put that back right now!! You two are driving me crazy. Get back over here right now."
Daughter:	"Mom, are you ready for a nap?"

Part III

Specific Problems

7

TREATMENT OF ANXIETY AND DEPRESSION

WHAT KIND OF THERAPY TO USE FOR THIS TYPE OF CHILD WITH THIS KIND OF PROBLEM

Play therapy is usually an integral part of the treatment of children aged preschool to early adolescence. A good treatment plan takes a multimodal approach: Using the most effective method(s) for the specific problems the child is experiencing.

Donald Keat's book *Child Multimodal Therapy* (1990) presents "an integrated look at the development of the multimodal approach" for assessment and child therapy. He describes multimodal therapy as a problem-solving approach that helps the therapist match the assessment with client treatment needs. "The main criteria for utilization is whether the techniques have been useful and helpful in therapeutic endeavors with children, adolescents, and their families. The primary questions are Does it work? Is it useful? Is it an effective therapeutic strategy?" (pp. 1–2)

Multimodal therapy techniques come from various theoretical orientations including behavioral, cognitive-behavioral, psychoanalytic, client-centered, developmental, and humanistic theories. (See Keat's book for more information on approaches and techniques of child multimodal therapy.)

Therapy is for the child. A skilled and caring play therapist will adapt the treatment to the specific needs of the child. This is particularly true when treatment averages six to twelve sessions as the majority of my cases do. This chapter focuses on the diagnostic categories of anxiety and depression. I recommend a multimodal approach using play therapy along with other techniques shown to be effective in treating this particular type of problem.

Example

A treatment plan for a child with separation anxiety would likely include:

- Play therapy in which the child expresses his fears and the therapist communicates understanding and coping with fear;
- Behavior therapy techniques such as relaxation training to teach the child how to reduce anxiety;
- Family therapy session(s) to assess and treat family dynamics that may have contributed to the development of separation anxiety, and

- Parent consultation in which parents are instructed in applying desensitization techniques.

TREATMENT OF ANXIETY

Case Example One—Separation Anxiety— Tommy, Seven-Year-Old Boy

Tommy was referred to me for treatment of severe separation anxiety and night time terrors. His parents reported that Tommy experienced panic reactions at home and in stores when a parent was out of sight. For example, Tommy could be playing in the yard at home with mother or dad. Tommy would turn to find a parent and if he didn't see one, he would immediately panic even though his parent was in the same yard. He had a similar reaction in stores if he looked and his mother or father could not immediately be seen.

Tommy was also afraid to spend time away from home at a friend's house. He had experienced separation anxiety in kindergarten but was coping reasonably well in the first grade, as long as there were predictable routines and structures. He relied on his mother to take him to school and pick him up.

Nighttime fears were persistent. Tommy was very reluctant to go to sleep at night. He awakened one or more times during the night, often from nightmares. Each time, he went to his parents' bedroom and slept on the floor next to his mother.

Tommy's treatment consisted of ten sessions. Family and parent interviews, the State-Trait Anxiety Inventory for Children (STAIC) and diagnostic play all confirmed the diagnosis of separation anxiety with panic reactions and nighttime terrors.

Using a multimodal approach, Tommy's treatment included:

- Family therapy and parent consultation. Both parents revealed experiences of childhood fears. Tommy's mother recalled the horror of a friend's young child who drowned in the family swimming pool when the child was briefly out of the mother's sight. She acknowledged her fears that something bad might happen to Tommy if she was not close by to protect him.
- Behavior therapy and cognitive behavior therapy for desensitization of fears. I used relaxation training for Tommy, fear hierarchy to identify specific fears, "facing fear" homework assignments, parent training in consistent night-time scheduling and comforting and returning Tommy to his room each time he awoke and came to his parents' bedroom.
- Play therapy for Tommy to express his separation fears and need for protection, and to gain some control over his fears. I used play as a reinforcer for improvement in "facing your fears." When his parents reported progress in fear reduction, I let Tommy choose a favorite activity. He enjoyed the Thinking, Feeling, Doing Game, and a pool-type Carrom game.

Sand tray play and storytelling techniques were very useful. In the second session, Tommy was active in sand tray play. He built fences to partition separate areas for his house, road and animals. I interpreted his play as his strong need for protection, sense of safety, and clear structure in his life. This was consistent with the reports that Tommy managed classroom activities and playing on sports teams without separation fears, but became anxious and panicky with minor changes in his routine.

Therapeutic storytelling was an effective means for Tommy to express his fears of harm coming to his family. I included desensitization of fears in my portion of storytelling.

In our sixth session, Tommy told this story:

Tommy's Story   "Godzilla's brother came and knocked this big building down and he had a real bad time, and that was my dream." Tommy was able to describe his scary dream.

Therapist's Story   "Once upon a time, there was this real neat kid who had a real bad dream, in which Godzilla's brother came and knocked down a big building. It was such a scary dream that it woke the boy. After that, he was afraid because he thought he would have a bad dream every night; it was real scary. Even in his own room, it was scary. But then, he had another dream, in which Godzilla's brother started shrinking. And he got smaller and smaller until he was just the size of a building. And he got smaller and smaller until he was the size of a house, and he got smaller and smaller until he was the size of a person, and he got smaller and smaller until he was the size of a kid, and he got smaller and smaller until he was the size of a puppy dog." Tommy spontaneously added to this desensitization story by saying that he got smaller and smaller until "he was just a baby."

Therapist: "Then he wasn't scared any more."

Tommy: "Somebody stepped on him."

Therapist: "So there was no more dream about him. The moral of the story is: Sometimes things start out awful, awful scary until they get smaller and smaller and they go away."

In this joint storytelling, Tommy dealt with his fears of someone breaking into his house.

Therapist: "Once upon a time, there was a bear by Tommy's house."

Tommy: "There was a bear. He tried to break in our house and I thought it was a bad guy. He came in and I was screaming to my Mom, and my Dad came up and stabbed him and he died. And I was so proud of my Dad, 'cause he's a good Dad."

Therapist: "The Dad protected him. It wasn't a person, it was a bear. How big a bear?"

Tommy: "Bigger than you."

Therapist: "So the next time someone came to the house and it was a . . . ."

Tommy: "It was a tiger."

Therapist: "Tiger came and . . . ."

Tommy: "He bited everybody in our house. And they took us to the emergency office. They fixed us up. And they killed the tiger. And they took us back home."

Therapist: "That was scary. Another day, somebody came to the house and it was a . . . "

Tommy: "Karate guy."

Therapist: "They didn't know if he was a good karate guy or a bad karate guy."

Tommy: "There was a good karate guy who chased the bad karate guy off. We finally woke up and we called 911. Karate guy came to our house and said, 'I took care of it.'"

Therapist: "That was good. That took care of that and then the next day, they wondered if anybody else would come and . . .."

Tommy: "The karate guy was still outside in case anybody else came. Then somebody came and it was a good person. He tried to karate him and we finally stopped him."

Therapist: "The karate guy didn't know he was a good guy and started to treat him like a bad person. But you stopped him."

Tommy:	"And it was my friend. And we told the karate guy, 'We're glad for you to protect us, but don't hurt any of our friends.'"
Therapist:	"What happened when the next one came?"
Tommy:	"The bad person decided to be a good person. And nobody came again."

Tommy was able to use joint storytelling to face his fears and to accept my suggestions that his fears could be reduced. By the tenth session, Tommy had slept in his own room for six weeks with only two nights when he came to his parents' bedroom, and one of those was a stormy night. His parents announced that he had stayed all night with a friend for the first time. Tommy told how he practiced relaxed breathing when he had anxious thoughts or feelings at home. He said, "I was brave."

Case Example Two—Adjustment Disorder with Anxiety—Kelly, Five-Year-Old Girl

Kelly was referred to me by her mother for anxiety symptoms of self abuse and anger outbursts of screaming, hitting, kicking at her two-year-old sister and, on occasion, at her mother. Kelly's parents had been divorced for one year. She lived with her mother and younger sister. Her father had standard visitation on every other weekend.

Kelly was seen for eight visits. The treatment of choice was play therapy and parent consultation with the mother. The father was not available for parent consultation.

Kelly was a bright, verbal, assertive girl who was active in therapy sessions. In the first session, she revealed her anxiety by drawing a picture of herself, her younger sister, and her grandmother "when I had a tornado and it rained." Kelly covered her family drawing with wild scrawls to show the storm. Kelly had been in a storm area four months earlier. Kelly's mother was concerned about her anxious and angry behavior after visitation with her father. There had been significant parent conflict about visitation over the past six months.

Kelly's drawing and the family and parent interviews indicated significant anxiety symptoms.

In the second session, I identified the reasons Kelly was coming to see me: Her fears, self-abuse of picking and scratching her forehead, anger and resistance toward her mother, and aggressive behavior toward her younger sister.

Kelly was responsive to play therapy opportunities. She was eager to play with many toys. Kelly usually took an assertive role in play therapy and played by "my rules."

In the third session, using clay and plastic animals, I introduced the theme of separation and divorce in a story about a young horse that moved to different places with bigger horses. Kelly quickly participated in this story. Kelly identified the old place where horses had lived and the new places. The old place was always cold; the new one was always hot. She liked the new place better. This indicated that Kelly was more comfortable with her present living arrangement with her mother and grandmother than with pre-divorce home conflicts.

At the beginning of each session, I checked with Kelly and her mother regarding progress in therapy goals of reducing anxiety, self-abuse and anger behavior. As she made progress, I used her choice of play activities as a reinforcer.

By the fourth session, Kelly showed no separation fear about leaving her mother in the reception room. She announced, "Dr. Price, I don't have anything to talk about . . . I want to play with the house today." Kelly used this and subsequent sessions to choose and explore the dollhouse, sand tray, puppets, play kitchen, and games with me.

Kelly's need for control of her environment was evident. Her changing daily schedule due to mother's work and to irregular visitation time with her father, created significant stress. She used play therapy to have control over her environment in a safe manner. Play therapy was an effective stress management program for her.

With her mother, I shared Kelly's need for structure, as much sameness as possible in her daily routine, clarity regarding the choices Kelly had or did not have in daily activities, and Kelly's need for play time with her mother and grandmother.

By the seventh session, Kelly's anxiety, self-abuse, and anger behavior had diminished significantly. I wanted to assess Kelly's ability to cope with present stress levels. In sand tray play, I introduced butterflies as being in danger from aggressive animals. Kelly took the role of protector of the butterflies. I interpreted this as a sign that Kelly felt strong instead of weak and helpless. This was consistent with her recent behavior in therapy and her mother's reports.

The same pattern was evident in the last session two weeks later. Kelly's mother reported "a great two weeks." Kelly chose to play with the doll house. She separated the girl and boy dolls and reversed the roles. Kelly was the boy; I was the girl. Her doll was brave, played with pet snakes and helped my doll not to fear snakes or pet lions.

Kelly drew me a "goodbye" picture of herself. It was made of bright colors and was age-appropriate. As she left, Kelly said, "I love you, Dr. Price." She hugged me goodbye in the reception room with her mother observing.

TREATMENT OF DEPRESSION

Case Example One—Adjustment Disorder with Depressed Mood—Rhonda, Ten-Year-Old Girl

Rhonda's depression was secondary to her referral problem of moderate to severe chronic headaches occurring daily for four weeks. Organic causes had been ruled out by her pediatrician and by a pediatric neurologist. Headaches were deemed to be psychosomatic in origin.

Rhonda was an attractive, slender girl of superior intelligence who excelled in school and was in a gifted and talented program. She lived with her biological parents and her twelve-year-old-brother. Her parents were very concerned and stressed about how to help their daughter with her severe headaches. She missed two of the past four weeks of school due to headaches. The previous school year, Rhonda had missed fifteen days due to headaches and stomachaches.

Rhonda's parents denied any serious family problems. Two stressors were reported in the past two years: The family move from out-of-state one year earlier was stressful for Rhonda and she still missed her old friends. Her mother's move to employment outside the home had created some stress for mother and daughter.

A multimodal treatment approach was used. Rhonda was seen for five sessions. Behavioral medicine treatment of relaxation training, guided imagery, record keeping, and thermal biofeedback were used for headache treatment. Play therapy was used for depression symptoms of withdrawal, fatigue, feelings of helplessness and anxiety, and increased dependence on parents.

In the third and fourth sessions, Rhonda was responsive to the techniques of mutual storytelling and continuous storytelling. (See Chapter Six, Page 99 for Rhonda as case example of Continuous Story variation of mutual storytelling.) I addressed her depression by introducing a story about Chipper the frog who lost his lively voice and became despondent.

Therapist: "Rhonda has been here two times before, but this is the first time we have done storytelling. The stories are to be made up from our own heads, not from a book or movie or any story we have

	heard. Rhonda, would you like the story to be about people or animals?"
Rhonda:	"Animals."
Therapist:	"I know that a frog is one of your favorite animals. Do you want the story to be about frogs or some other animal?"
Rhonda:	"Frogs."
Therapist:	"Okay. Once upon a time, way off in the forest, far, far away, there was a big pond with lily pads on it, trees around it for shade; there were sunny areas, and fish. There were a good number of frogs. One was named Chipper, which was an unusual name for a frog. This frog had a high- pitched voice that sounded like 'Ribet! Ribet! Ribet!' Everybody knew Chipper because of her special sound and because she could jump and swim really well. Chipper was always full of energy, singing and hopping." (This was to describe how talented Rhonda was and how well she usually did until the headaches and depressed mood occurred.) "Somehow, Chipper lost her voice. Instead, she made a low, sad sound of 'Croak, croak, croak.' The other frogs asked, 'What's wrong with Chipper?' They started giving her a lot of advice of 'Just do it this way so you can get your voice back.'" (This was a reference to all the medical care and family concern she had recently received.) "But, it didn't

work and Chipper got so *discouraged* and quit swimming a lot, stayed on the bank, and was unhappy. Everybody was really worried about Chipper. But then, the summer came, the sun came out, and an old, old frog came and said, 'I think it's just something in your throat. Let's just give you some special food and gradually see if your voice will come back.'" (Introduction of hope and recent progress.) "And they did, and her voice went from soft 'Ribet' to strong 'Ribet!' to STRONG and LOUD 'RIBET! RIBET!' And Chipper became Chipper again. And all the other frogs watched her do all the things she liked to do. The moral of the story is sometimes you don't understand when bad things happen, and it sure helps when you regain what you've lost. The end."

Rhonda followed with her story.

Rhonda: "Once there was a frog named Greenie. Greenie was very unusual because she was always reading a book." (Rhonda identified with Greenie because they both loved to read.) "But one day all her books were gone. One of her best friends, Frenchie, had all her books and was eating them fast because she was so hungry. Greenie got very mad at Frenchie because she hadn't asked permission and

those were Greenie's favorite books."
(Rhonda's character expressed anger at
her loss of enjoyment of books. This was
her most direct acknowlegement of her
own disappointment, anger and sadness
regarding peer relations.) "So Frenchie
felt very bad and got this terrible stomachache from eating all the paper and
glue and stuff. (Here Rhonda expresses
a desire to get even with a friend.) She
finally went to Greenie and said, 'Will
you forgive me?' Greenie said, 'Yes, but
you have to promise me you won't eat
anything except what you are supposed
to.' Frenchie said, 'Okay.' The end.

I guess the moral is, Greenies never get
what they want." (Rhonda's story ended
with the acceptance there is give and
take in making and keeping friends.)

Therapist: I followed this with a more direct story.
Rhonda and I used a continuous story
approach. "Once there was this child
who liked to climb mountains, read, and
really liked to learn. But something happened, and took away some of the enjoyment. And the problem was . . .."
Rhonda's story was about a child who
became angry at her parents and her
friends, refused to talk with them, kept
her mad more and more to herself and
even refused to talk with her friends.
Rhonda spoke of the parents bringing

the child to a special doctor to help kids with problems. The girl began talking and told him all about her life. At the end of the story, Rhonda said, "She was nice again . . . talked to her parents . . . got used to it."

Therapist: "That's the story about how the girl learned to cope with something so hard."

Play therapy with storytelling was an effective treatment for Rhonda's depression. She was able to tell her story of anger, fear and sadness, gain release from depression, and begin to use her coping ability to reduce headaches and regain enjoyment of school. Rhonda's behavioral medicine treatment continued and after six weeks her headaches were gone.

In the fourth session, Rhonda used clay to make "Greenie" the frog and acted out a story of adventure, danger, friendship, separation from home and return. She used the story to express her desire for more control over her life, her dependence-independence conflict regarding her parents, her need for friendship and her increased ability to cope with headaches.

In the fifth and final session, Rhonda was animated in talking about her interests in school, art, and having a very full schedule of activities.

I used "Complete a Story" for termination time. The story theme was about a family of goats who lost their ability and interest in climbing, but regained them to enjoy climbing high mountains again.

Case Example Two—Dysthymia (Depression)— Earl, Six-Year-Old Boy

Earl was referred by his parents and his family's pastor for recent depressive statements, a history of mood swings, self-criticism and low self esteem. The immediate parent concerns were Earl's statements that he didn't care if he lived or died. He also had said, "I'm the dumbest person in the world."

Earl lived with his biological parents and his five-year-old sister. He was enrolled in the first grade. His parents reported that Earl had high expectations of himself and became quite upset when he didn't do as well as he thought he should on school assignments.

My diagnostic assessment confirmed clinical depression with a diagnosis of Dysthymia. The duration of his depression symptoms was two years: His parents reported a significant change in Earl's temperament in the past two years. Although his mother had a history of depression and had taken an antidepressant, she stopped taking it one year before Earl's treatment began. She reported other relatives with a history of depression.

Earl was assessed at High Average Intellectual ability, high social needs, emotionally expressive, and a child with a rich, active fantasy life. His parents, in contrast, tended to be emotionally constricted and were having a difficult time understanding Earl's strong moods and dramatic temperament.

Using a multimodal approach that included family systems theory, I made the following recommendations:

- Individual therapy for Earl that included play therapy for depression and self-esteem problems, behavior therapy for anxiety and anger, that included relaxation training, affective education for recognition of his positive and negative moods, and anger management training.
- Family therapy that included joint sessions with all four family members and regular parent consultation to improve his parents' ability to understand and assist their talented and troubled six-year-old. Earl's mother felt guilty for her son's problems and hated that Earl "is just like I was as a child."
- For the mother to consider psychotherapy for her depression and to consult with her physician regarding her need for an antidepressant.

Earl and his family were seen for twelve sessions. Earl was responsive to relaxation training and anger management. He set goals:

1. "Get along with my five-year-old sister."
2. "If I get mad, get over it, and not get in trouble with Mom and Dad."

In the early sessions, I focused on Earl's fears: his separation anxiety regarding his father's frequent business travel that kept him away from home overnight, and his autonomy conflicts, particularly with his mother, and on his anger behavior.

Earl responded well to play therapy sessions. He used drawings and clay to express his anger and aggressive impulses. In his Kinetic Family Drawing, Earl omitted his parents and drew himself, his sister and two cousins. His house drawing was of his aunt and uncle's home rather than his family. (These drawings indicated significant anger and opposition toward parents.) Earl omitted facial features on his initial drawings (indication of pathology). His difficulty in managing his strong emotions were also suggested in his early drawings. Earl drew a "robot with a human face." He also identified with his "alien" drawing.

Earl expressed his aggressive and hostile impulses by drawing dinosaurs and making a clay dinosaur with which he acted out an aggressive story. When I asked Earl what animal he would like to be, he said, "a werewolf because they're mean; they're cool."

As Earl expressed more of his anger and aggression in play therapy, his parents reported a decrease in anger and oppositional behavior at home and school. Earl was quite creative. In one session, he brought his "invention" of a car that he had designed. At another session, Earl brought a homemade card to show me. These were good indicators that he had formed a relationship with me and felt comfortable in sharing his creative projects, as well as his suppressed anger.

In family sessions, Earl's mother and father became more comfortable in complimenting and in responding to their son's creative play, love of fantasy and storytelling. They participated in parent-child play activities to a lesser degree. In parent counseling, I addressed the mother's avoidance of conflict and her frustration with having a son with strong verbal skills who enjoyed arguments, and who had high control needs, the importance of his father playing with his son, and the need for consistent parenting based on their son's need for clear structure.

At the end of therapy, both parents reported that Earl's behavior was "satisfactory" at school and home. Earl's mother had seen her physician and been placed on an antidepressant; she was considering psychotherapy for herself. Earl's father said both he and his wife "understood Earl better" and felt they had improved in knowing how to parent him, and how to better manage behavior problems when they occurred.

PRACTICAL EXERCISE

Using a multimodal approach, develop treatment plans for children with a diagnosis of anxiety and/or depression.

1. Select a case with anxiety diagnosis.
    Description of Child:

    Specific Problem(s) Treatment Plans:

    Progress and Comments:

2. Select a case with depression diagnosis.
   Description of Child:

   Specific Problem(s):

   Treatment Plans: Progress and Comments:

CHILDQUOTE

Guilty, Not Guilty

Five-year-old Kerry had just been diagnosed with Attention Deficit Hyperactivity Disorder (ADHD). I had his father read the book *Shelley, the Hyperactive Turtle* to Kerry to help him understand what ADHD was. When Kerry's dad read the section describing how Shelley couldn't keep still, was constantly squirming, and was often in trouble for not paying attention, Kerry turned to me and said, "Dr. Price, that's me." But when his father read the part about how Shelley got in trouble at mealtimes by playing with his food and throwing it, Kerry declared in a serious tone of voice, "But I don't throw *food!*"

Not To Worry

Five-year-old Sean had made significant improvement in therapy. His parents reported fewer anger outbursts, a decrease in behavior problems and improved cooperation with parents. Sean told his therapist, "Sometimes me and Mom argue. Don't worry about that. We'll get over it."

8

TREATMENT OF BEHAVIOR PROBLEMS

WHAT KIND OF THERAPY TO USE FOR THIS TYPE OF CHILD WITH THIS KIND OF PROBLEM

This chapter focuses on the use of a multimodal approach in the treatment of behavior problems.

Case Example One—Adjustment Disorder with Disturbance of Conduct—Adam, Eight-Year-Old Boy

Adam was a muscular boy and the oldest of four children. He was adopted as an infant and had three sisters ages seven, two, and two weeks. The stressors in the family included major conflict between parents and grandparents, adjustment to a newborn in the home, and recent concerns about being adopted.

Behavior problems included physically aggressive behavior at school, disobedience to his teacher's commands, disobedience to his parents (especially his adoptive mother), anger and physical aggression toward his seven-year-old and two-year-old sisters, and lying. Adam had a negative self concept. He said that he often got mad at himself for getting in trouble at home and at school.

The diagnostic interview revealed that the family was emotionally stressed, particularly due to an estrangement between the parents and the maternal grandparents who had been very involved in the children's lives. The father worked out of town several days each month. Adam's mother was frustrated with him for being a difficult child to parent and for his power struggle with her strict family rules.

I developed a multimodal treatment approach that included family therapy, parent consultation, individual therapy for Adam and a behavior management plan. I also provided individual therapy for Adam's mother.

Adam's play therapy treatment goals were:

1. Improving his poor self concept. He thought of himself as often "in trouble."
2. Managing anger and reducing his aggressive behavior at school and home. Adam told me, "I have trouble with obedience."
3. Dealing with Adam's concerns about being adopted.
4. Meeting some of Adam's autonomy needs for more control over his life.

In his projective drawings, Adam expressed his desire for more independence. His drawing of himself contained the statement, "He's happy to have time by himself." He said, "I like to play a lot." His play included aggressive themes such as army battles. He spoke of liking *GI Joe* on television, then commented that his parents wouldn't let him watch such programs.

Adam revealed some insight into his problems. He said, "Sometimes I'd like for you and me to drink a Coke, and just sit down and talk about my problems. I've got a bunch of 'em." Adam was eager for some individual play therapy time. Treatment consisted of nine sessions, four of which were family therapy and parent consultation. His parents limited the number of sessions due to financial concerns.

Parent consultation focused on their understanding Adam's strong need for more autonomy, having clear rules with less emphasis on punishment, and placing more emphasis on earning privileges. We developed a token economy program in which Adam's parents reinforced his cooperative behavior and control of aggression. In play therapy, I set conditions so that Adam earned choices in play contingent upon his compliance with my rules. Adam responded well to clear limits and consequences.

Adam's progress was largely due to his parents' implementing the token economy program and their willingness to understand the needs of their strong-willed and oppositional son. Play therapy contributed by providing a safe setting in which Adam could express his frustration and aggressive impulses within clear limits. He responded well to having his therapist listen to his problems and play with him.

When therapy was terminated by his parents, Adam had made moderate improvement regarding noncompliance and arguing with them. He had opportunity to discuss his concerns about his biological mother with his adoptive parents. There was a mild reduction in power struggles with his mother. School behavior improved to a moderate degree.

With a disturbance-of-conduct diagnosis, a child like Adam needs clear, appropriate rules with consistent implementation of consequences. Behavior modification principles are useful in such treatment. Parent and school consultation and behavior monitoring is needed. Letting a child have time to express aggressive impulses in an acceptable manner is helpful. The key is helping the parents better understand their child and how to provide parenting based on the child's needs.

Case Example Two—Oppositional Defiant Disorder (ODD)—Riley, Four-Year-Old Girl

Riley was a very verbal girl of above-average intellectual ability. Her parents divorced when Riley was one year old. She lived with her biological mother, sixteen-year-old brother and one-year-old brother. She had weekly visitation with her biological father.

Diagnostic play and parent consultation revealed Oppositional Defiant Disorder characteristics: Riley often argued with adults, refused to comply with adults' rules, was assertive and dominating, and frequently lost her temper.

Riley was described by her mother as strong-willed. "She will just tell you 'no' and refuse to do what she's told." Her mother viewed Riley as "free-spirited, like a little Mustang pony pulling at the reins." Behaviors included periodic severe temper tantrums at day care and home that lasted up to forty-five minutes.

In our first two sessions, Riley presented with a dependence versus independence conflict. Assertive in the activities she wanted to do, she usually took the dominant role in play therapy. By contrast, Riley exhibited dependence on her mother, wanting her mother not to leave the clinic room. Riley still slept with her mother and demanded a baby bottle at night.

Riley, as many children with an Oppositional Defiant Disorder diagnosis (ODD) do, had other presenting problems. Separation anxiety was a major concern. Riley exhibited excessive attachment to her mother, and anger and lack of trust toward her father. Separation anxiety and anger reactions occurred more frequently at day care.

What kind of treatment was best for Riley with the ODD and separation anxiety diagnoses? My treatment plan included:

1. Regular consultation with Riley's mother to help her understand her strong-willed child, and for treatment of the separation anxiety, temper outbursts, and power struggles.
2. Periodic consultation with Riley's father to reduce

her ambivalent feelings of love and fear toward him.

3. Consultation with day care teachers for child management.

4. Play therapy with Riley to address her strong autonomy needs, her independence versus dependence conflict, and to help her develop trust in adult males. Play therapy provided a setting in which her assertiveness was permitted within limits. A benefit of play therapy with such a child is that it gives her more control within the context of limited choices. For Riley's mother, I demonstrated methods for parenting her charming and challenging daughter.

I saw Riley for twenty-one sessions over a fifteen-month period. She was fun to work with. Riley had definite ideas of the toys she wanted to use: Puppets, the doll house, clay, animals and drawings were her preference. Riley used therapy to establish a trusting relationship with a father figure.

In the fourth session, Riley expressed some of her fears. She built a clay volcano that frightened her two play hippos. I addressed Riley's need for safety and protection by helping her build a clay cave for the hippos. (Riley feared her father because of past experiences of hearing his loud voice and seeing her mother terrified by her dad's anger. She had strong emotional reactions to loud voices.)

Riley responded to her fears by changing the volcano (unpredictable danger) to a protective wall for her animals. In the next session of puppet play, Riley expressed her anger at her father. Riley told him she was real mad at him because he yelled at her and hit her mother. Anger replaced Riley's fear.

Riley addressed her oppositional and demanding behavior toward her mother in subsequent sessions which we monitored and dealt with in each session. I recommended use of limited choices when Riley made strong demands. Temper tantrums at home and school were discussed. With clay and animals, Riley was able to express her aggression and move toward some control. Drama and dance classes provided creative outlets for Riley's artistic temperament.

By the last session, at age five, Riley dictated a letter to her father along with a drawing that expressed her fear and love for him. Compliance at kindergarten and day care improved; Riley was positive about her teacher. Tantrums at home and school were infrequent.

Attention Deficit Hyperactivity Disorder (ADHD)

The treatments of choice for ADHD—primarily Inattentive Type, primarily Impulsive-Hyperactive type, or Combined type, are behavior modification and medication: Psychostimulants or antidepressants. More than one-half of Attention Deficit Disorder (ADD) patients have additional clinical issues. Depression, anxiety, oppositional defiant disorder, negative self concept or peer relationship problems are often present. Play therapy is not the primary therapy for ADD children, but it can be helpful as part of a multimodal treatment.

**Case Example Three—Attention Deficit Disorder—
Bobby, Nine-Year-Old Boy**

Bobby was referred by his teachers and parents for aggressive behavior problems. His parents had doubts whether their son really had ADHD. Developmental history and teacher and parent checklists were significant for ADHD, primarily Impulsive-Hyperactive type. Diagnostic play with Bobby yielded significant information regarding his identity as a child with strong aggressive impulses and impulsiveness who needed to learn self control.

In play with clay people and animals, Bobby quickly took the role of an alligator that lived in a swamp. His alligator was active and impulsive; it bit a boy and fought any other animals that approached it.

I introduced the idea of setting limits. I began building a zoo with a fenced area to contain the alligator. Bobby joined me in constructing the zoo. I introduced a zoo keeper (therapist) who taught the alligator how to control himself. Bobby then made a leash for the alligator and took him back to the swamp where he had the leash for control. (I interpreted this as his school environment where limits were needed.) Thus in a thirty-minute session, Bobby identified his most serious ADHD symptoms: Impulsivity, irritability, arguing, and fighting. He accepted my role as teacher-helper and presented a hopeful prognosis for improvement.

**Case Example Four—Attention Deficit
Hyperactivity Disorder—Kerry, Five-Year-Old Boy**

Use of bibliotherapy, play therapy, and behavior therapy.

Kerry was a bright preschooler who met the criteria for ADHD. His father had a difficult time academically in school and was diagnosed with ADHD as an adult. I wanted Kerry to understand hyperactivity. I had his father read him the book *Shelley the Hyperactive Turtle* (1989) by Deborah M. Moss. His dad's participation in bibliotherapy helped Kerry understand his ADHD and ways the therapist and his family could help.

Kerry sat beside his dad looking at the pictures while his dad read. The book describes a young turtle that squirms, wiggles, can't sit still and gets in a lot of trouble, behavior that Kerry's parents had used to describe him. Kerry told his Dad, "That's me." On a page that shows Shelly in a food fight with other turtles, Kerry said to his dad, "*But, I* don't throw *food.*" Through bibliotherapy, Dad helped his son understand his ADHD and ways to be helped.

During storytelling, I told about a boy named Curious, who was in trouble a lot for not minding and for getting into things. Kerry blurted out, "Dr. Max, that's me."

Kerry's parents were responsive to guidance and parent education. They added more structure to his schedule, asked preschool teachers to provide daily feedback on his behavior, and set up a point system so that Kerry could earn privileges. After two consecutive sessions in which his parents reported much improvement in preschool and home behavior, we did this joint storytelling.

Child: "A kid was walking along and there was a big volcano with fire."

Therapist: "And the kid was frightened by the fire."

Child: "And he ran to his parents."

Therapist: "Then, the next time he was walking and . . .."

Child: "This time the volcano was just a bunch of rocks."

Therapist: "And the kid wasn't scared or mad anymore. Boys and girls, Kerry used to be like a volcano with fire, but now he has done so well in preschool and at home, he's not so hyperactive. Kerry, the boys and girls want to know how they can get better if they are hyperactive."

Child: "Be good and control your mad."

Kerry accepted my interpretation of his story and my direct statements about his having ADHD.

Case Example Four—Learning Disability and ADHD—Don, Eight-Year-Old Boy

Use of behavior therapy, psychostimulant medication, play therapy, consultation with parent and teacher.

Don was referred to me for a psychological evaluation due to poor academic performance at school. The evaluation yielded a diagnosis of Learning Disorder of Written Expression, Adjustment Disorder with Mixed Anxiety and Depressed Mood, and ADHD-primarily Inattentive type.

I began with behavior therapy and school consultation for Don's learning disability, memory and concentration problems. His parents were reluctant to use medication for ADHD symptoms.

For problems of loneliness from lack of friends, somatic complaints of stomach pain, and nighttime anxiety symptoms, I used play therapy, relaxation training and parent consultation.

In six sessions, Don made mild progress with ADHD symptoms of distractibility, forgetfulness, short attention span, and physical restlessness. His school teacher adjusted his classroom instruction for his mild learning disability of written expression and ADHD. Don's mother maintained regular contact with his teacher and monitored his homework.

In therapy, Don was activity-oriented. He had difficulty in talking about his concerns. Don complained that his father had little time to play with him and "yelled" at times. He responded positively to play therapy in which I was a father figure. Don's preferred play media were clay, in which he enjoyed the physical sensations of molding and building space themes of planets and robots, and projective drawings in which he expressed anxiety, suppressed anger, and desire for more power in his life. He also preferred active games in which he progressed from the control of Win level to improved social skills of interaction and mild risk taking of the CHANCE level (for psycho-social levels, see Chapter Three).

When Don continued to have significant ADHD symptoms despite behavior modification treatment, his parents agreed to a medication trial. Don responded positively to a psychostimulant and continued behavior treatment.

I used relaxation training, including making Don an audio tape to use at night for his nighttime anxiety. Don was sensitive to noise and was particularly bothered at nighttime by extraneous sounds. The audio tape provided white noise that drowned out night noises and "helps me go to sleep."

After twelve sessions that covered one year, treatment was terminated. Don was successful academically and socially at school, and his emotional problems were at non-clinical levels. He had several friends and an improved relationship with his father. Don's mother reported his overall adjustment was good, and he was making excellent progress in his grades with mostly As on his report card. A subsequent follow up three months later reported that Don continued to maintain good adjustment in his school work.

Case Example Six—Oppositional Defiant Disorder (ODD) and Attention Deficit Hyperactivity Disorder (ADHD)—Jason, Six-Year-Old Boy

Jason lived with his adoptive parents and his adopted ten-year-old sister. He was a handsome boy, short in stature. He had large brown eyes, and was very active and aggressive in our initial sessions.

Jason was referred for severe behavior problems in first grade that occurred on a daily basis. Typical classroom management techniques did little to decrease his aggressive and oppositional behavior. The school was ready to evaluate Jason for possible placement in a class for the severe emotionally disturbed (SED). His dad was angry at the school and at Jason for refusing to obey his mother and his female teacher. Jason's mother was very distressed at Jason's behavior and felt she was a failure as his parent.

ADHD was diagnosed from a clinical interview, classroom observation, a parent interview, and ADHD checklists. Jason responded positively to a psychostimulant. His hyperactivity, impulsiveness, and aggression decreased. He was able to stay in the regular classroom and achieve at grade level.

Jason's behavior problems decreased from severe to moderate. Parent and school consultation continued with emphasis on the use of behavior modification principles. A daily school behavior report card addressed specific problems of cooperation with his teacher, not hitting other students and completing assignments. Jason earned home privileges based on his daily school behavior. He averaged two days a week with no serious behavior problems at school.

Play therapy addressed Jason's aggression, fears and oppositional behaviors. He was eager for time to play with clay and plastic animals, acting out original stories. He liked to have his stories recorded on audio tape. Jason often repeated the same theme from one session to the next.

The following is an example of Jason's play therapy with therapeutic storytelling that extended through three sessions. The pattern progressed from generalized physical aggression to decreased aggression to controlled aggression; from aggression toward peers to social contact, to friendship.

Therapist:	"Good morning, boys and girls. Welcome to Dr. Price's storytelling time. My special guest is Jason. Say hello to the boys and girls."
Child:	"Hello. We forgot to tell them about the animals" (in reference to last session's story).
Therapist:	"Yes. Last time, we had an animal story that didn't get finished. Would you like to hear the whole story?"
Child:	"YES!! The animal story. The story is going to be about the man that is trying to catch his food."

Jason took several minutes to build a forest with trees, grass and a house for the man. Jason's story began with the man hunting for animals in the forest. He identified with the animals' fears and anger toward the hunter.

Jason next took the role of King Lion who controlled the other animals in the forest. He was very animated as he acted out fights using a forceful voice.

When I introduced the theme of controlled aggression by having the lion forceful only when threatened or searching for food, Jason resisted. His classic comment was "It's hard to be King of the Jungle if animals aren't afraid of you."

At this point, he had difficulty with any role other than dominance or deception. Jason's self concept was one of being a "bad kid" who was difficult to manage. Dominating his environment reinforced him.

In the next story, Jason's theme was mental aggression. He acted out a story of a leprechaun who tricked a boy who was trying to steal his gold. Jason identified with the leprechaun. The moral of his story was, "Leprechauns are tricky."

I responded with the following story to address Jason's oppositional behavior toward his peers.

Therapist: "Once upon a time, there was this leprechaun that was always tricking people. He also began to trick other leprechauns. After a while they said, 'You're not our friend anymore' and he was all by himself. When he wanted other leprechauns to help him get more gold, they wouldn't do it."

"So, the leprechaun said, 'Okay, I won't trick my friends anymore. I'll only trick bad people who are trying to hurt me, or get my gold.'

From then on, he didn't trick as many people. Just the bad people, and he had more friends. The end. The moral of the story is, don't trick your friends."

My purpose in this story was to introduce the concept of discriminating when to use and not use his "me against the world" view of social contact.

I saw mild progress when Jason moved from an aggressive lion role to a protective role. He identified with strong animals that stood up to a bullying giraffe and rescued the animal babies.

Jason continued aggressive themes in his play and storytelling for several more sessions. His progress was slow and inconsistent, with a controlled aggression theme one moment, followed by physical aggression and dominating themes.

Three months later, Jason progressed to a more selective expression of his aggressive impulses and increased cooperation.

This joint storytelling is an example:

Therapist: "Boys and girls, today we are going to tell a story about the lion that we used to talk about. There was a lion who wanted to be King of the Jungle.

He went around roaring, chasing and biting all the other animals until they were afraid of him."

Child: "And he ended up with no friends."

Therapist: "Because no one wants to be friends with someone they are afraid of and who hurts them."

Child: "And that story ends up with not to be mean to people if you want to be friends."

Therapist:	"Right. So the lion found some other ways to act."
Child:	"He started being nice to the other animals."
Therapist:	"They said, 'Wow, you have really changed. We like having a strong friend. We know if we need protection, you'll be there. You can run fast and teach us things.'" (I introduced the twin themes of being strong and being friendly).
Child:	"The lion helped the small animals."
Therapist:	"He learned to use fighting only to protect the small animals."

The use of play therapy and behavior therapy was successful in reducing the amount of Jason's aggressive behavior and helping him to make some friends.

Conduct Disorder

Conduct Disorders are difficult cases that require multimodal treatment. Long-term treatment is recommended. Goals are designed to manage aggressive behavior and serious violation of rules. Progress is measured in minor improvements and prevention of further aggressive behavior. I have found children with Conduct Disorder very challenging to work with. A caring and understanding therapist is not sufficient: Firmness, consistency and directness are necessary.

Case Example Seven—Childhood Onset Conduct Disorder—Jeremy, Five-and-a-Half to Nine-Year-Old Boy

Jeremy was five-and-a-half years old when I first met him. He was seen for severe behavior problems including verbal and physical aggression toward peers, threats of killing himself with a knife, and threats of hurting his family. Jeremy's parents had recently divorced. He lived in crowded conditions with his mother, maternal grandparents and four sisters ages two, four, ten and eleven.

Jeremy was referred to me for treatment after he received an outpatient diagnostic assessment at a local children's clinic.

Jeremy's background information was disturbing. He lived in a dysfunctional family without a positive attachment to any parent figure. Jeremy had been abused for several years by his biological father. His mother was hospitalized shortly after his birth and had been in a psychiatric hospital for bi-polar disorder for five months during the previous year. Jeremy and his sisters lived with their maternal grandmother during their mother's absence. The grandmother was described as harsh and nonnurturing.

The psychologist's report concluded that Jeremy was "A seriously emotionally disturbed child who has been both physically and emotionally abused over a number of years." In addition, Jeremy had encopresis (a soiling disorder), hyperactivity and developmental delays.

How do you treat a child like Jeremy when the

prognosis is poor? You give the treatment you can give. I saw him periodically for four years. His diagnoses were: Conduct Disorder, Attention-Deficit Hyperactivity Disorder, Separation Anxiety, Functional Encopresis, Developmental Articulation Disorder, Parent-Child Problem—severe.

I referred Jeremy for inpatient treatment after four sessions, due to the severity of his problems and continuing home and school crises. He was in residential treatment for seven months. I saw Jeremy and his mother for therapy while he was in residential treatment with the goal of returning to his mother.

During his kindergarten year, treatment consisted of:

- Consultation with school, residential treatment staff, and with his mother.
- Monitoring of ADHD behavior and psychostimulant treatment.
- Behavior treatment plan for managing severe behavior problems and for encopresis.
- Play therapy with Jeremy and joint sessions with Jeremy and his mother.

Jeremy responded to play therapy when I provided predictable and consistent limits. He formed an alliance of cooperation/resistance with me. In some play sessions, he identified with me as his "buddy." He displayed gentleness in taking the role of protector of a plastic puppy. Jeremy acted out his aggression toward the therapist and scary animals with play guns, but Jeremy demonstrated some self-control of his aggressiveness when he was in the predictable therapy setting.

There was no close attachment between mother and child. Jeremy's mother showed periods of concern for Jeremy, but her own health problems and pathology, and her limited parenting skills, prevented mother-son bonding and affection.

A typical session with Jeremy would begin with loud, boisterous behavior. I would introduce relaxation training with material reinforcers for cooperation. Jeremy would respond to this structure, and use thirty minutes to express his concerns of the day: Sometimes anger or resistance toward the therapist; sometimes fears, sometimes caring behavior. My role was to be the consistent person in his life, one he could count on to be there, to set clear limits, and be genuine with him.

Jeremy returned home to live with his mother to begin first grade and made some progress. He responded positively to a psychostimulant for ADHD; he was in a class for emotionally disturbed children, and his school adjustment was fair. Jeremy responded to a token system of behavior management. Home life continued to be unpredictable: His mother was in the hospital again that year, and was injured in a car accident. His grandmother or mother parented him, whichever one was available.

Jeremy received two months of "excellent" and "very good" behavior reports from school and home when his mother was actively involved in his care. Jeremy expressed some pride in his behavior; he was calmer and in a more pleasant mood. In joint play sessions with his mother, there was some attachment behavior including hugging, both tolerated and initiated by Jeremy. He was resistive to his mother initiating hugging unless he desired it. Still, this was a significant breakthrough in parent-child relations.

Jeremy's behavior problems were fewer during the rest of his first-grade year. He finished the year in a class for the severely emotional disturbed (SED) half the day, and was mainstreamed for half the day. His achievement was near grade level. His soiling disorder improved, but there was one serious incident of playing with fire at home.

Jeremy began second grade with satisfactory school behavior. In play therapy, he repeated his theme of being a rescuer, saving children from a fire. He was considerate of his three-year-old sister with whom he had been aggressive. His anger was reduced.

Anxiety was the dominant theme in Jeremy's play. Despite continued family stress, Jeremy made mild improvement in his behavioral and emotional problems of anxiety and depression. Then his family moved out of town, and I didn't hear from them for fifteen months.

I saw Jeremy again for one year from ages eight-and-a-half to nine-and-a-half, until he was admitted to a day treatment program. Prior to seeing me at age eight-and-a- half, Jeremy was an inpatient at a local psychiatric hospital for two months. The hospital's final diagnosis was:

- Attention Deficit Hyperactivity Disorder-severe
- Dysthymia (depression)

- Conduct Disorder, solitary aggressive type
- Functional encopresis

Jeremy was in the third grade when he resumed therapy. He did well in the SED class most of the year. He experienced encopresis almost daily. He did improve with the same behavior therapy I previously used, and the soilings reduced to once a week. His family situation was still chaotic. Jeremy's mother was inconsistent in keeping appointments. Jeremy had had no contact with his biological father in two-and-a-half years. There was no attachment to this abusive father. I recommended to the mother that Jeremy have a male role model in activities such as Boy Scouts, Big Brothers or organized sports.

Jeremy responded to play therapy during the second semester of the third grade. Mutual storytelling was often used. These are some of his play themes:

- In one puppet play session, Jeremy began with aggressive puppets controlling the forests; later, the lion puppet made the forest safe for other puppets. His play began with aggression, then animals escaping from aggression and finding a safe place. The puppet returned to the past frightening setting and faced it with less aggression. This was a good description of Jeremy's life in which he had experienced fear and aggression, had found times when he was safer, but now was faced with a similar chaotic situation.
- One storytelling theme was about a hunter killing animals. My theme of controlled aggression had the hunter killing only for food.

- One story dealt with frequent separation from home. I told a story of a parrot that became angry at its new owners, referring to his recent hospitalization. Jeremy's story was that the parrot was angry at the pet store owner until "he got back with his real family," and the parrot was okay.

- One story theme was of distrust. Jeremy used the Three Little Pigs story theme with his account that "the three pigs were given poison food from the witch." Jeremy was unable to trust that his need to be nurtured would be met by his mother figures.

Jeremy had a considerate, thoughtful side that was seen occasionally in therapy.

But, his home environment was so predictably inconsistent, and his behavioral and emotional problems so severe, that he was unable to cope well for any significant time period.

The family moved in the summer and he began the fourth grade in a different school. Jeremy's behavioral problems increased. Aggressive play themes were dominant. He wanted to change schools and go to a day treatment program that was like previous residential programs. In the fall of his fourth grade year, Jeremy made a suicidal gesture at home by tying a jump rope around his neck. I referred him for residential treatment and had no further contact with Jeremy after that.

Jeremy's story is an example of the difficulty of working with a seriously disturbed child when the home resources are not available or adequate for him.

Case Example Eight—Conduct Disorder-Group Type, Adolescent Onset and Dysthymia (Depression)—Kristy, Eleven Years, Two Months to Fifteen Years, Eleven Months-Old

When I first met Kristy, she was eleven years old. She came to the first session neatly dressed and well groomed, wearing makeup. Her appearance was that of a hurried child trying to grow up too fast. Kristy was polite, serious minded, talked in a grown-up voice, and made obvious efforts to please me. Her presenting problems were attention-getting behavior problems at school and symptoms of depression.

Kristy's background information was very significant. She had lived with her maternal uncle, Gary, and her aunt, Gwen, since she was seven, after her mother was killed by a relative. She was adopted by this uncle and aunt. The family constellation included an eighteen-year-old biological brother plus Gary and Gwen's seventeen-year-old daughter and thirteen-year-old son. Kristy's maternal grandparents lived nearby and were a significant part of her life. Kristy's adoptive parents described her personality as "pleasant and outgoing to people she isn't around all the time, but resistive and argumentative with family and people she is often around." They were concerned that Kristy was becoming a manipulator like her deceased biological mother.

My initial assessment identified depression with unresolved grief, periodic behavior problems at school, including conflicts with peers and disagreements with teachers, along with some lying and stealing behavior. Recurrent dreams of her mother's tragic death were symptoms of her post-traumatic stress disorder.

Seeing Kristy at different times over a four-and-a-half year period provided a picture of how she moved from depression and periodic behavior problems to conduct disorder in early adolescence.

What kind of treatment would be best for Kristy? I recommended individual therapy for Kristy, family therapy and parent consultation every other session, and behavior therapy for school behavior problems. The family agreed to my recommendations, but I saw her only twice a month since the family lived out of town. The treatment pattern was one in which Kristy would respond to treatment, behavior problems and depression would improve, therapy would stop for a few months at her parents' request, then begin again when behavior problems resurfaced.

The treatment goals for the first year were:

1. Decrease depression through grief therapy related to her mother's violent death four years earlier.
2. Increase attachment and a sense of belonging to her adoptive family, particularly her Aunt Gwen and her siblings.
3. Develop a behavior management program for her underachievement and social conflicts at school.

Significant progress was noted in the first six months. Kristy's grades improved to As and Bs and her relationship with her family enhanced. She was able to talk about the events and recurring dreams of being present when her mother was killed. Kristy requested and visited her mother's grave, for the first time in two years. She was less pessimistic about school. She played on the school basketball team and enjoyed piano lessons. Kristy was able to verbalize her emotions and problems. She spoke of never knowing who her biological father was. She described her pain as "feeling empty inside."

Play therapy techniques to which Kristy responded included projective drawings, play with clay and plastic animals, and puppet play with mutual storytelling.

One of Kristy's drawings and stories in the first two months of treatment was particularly biographical. She drew a picture of a puppy that was locked up in an animal shelter. Her drawing included a female person standing outside the animal cage. Kristy said, "this person locked up this pound puppy 'cause it was out in the street without a collar. The puppy is in a cage at the vet's. Something bad will happen to it. A person might kill the puppy 'cause nobody will buy it." I interpreted the drawing as Kristy identifying with the pound puppy feeling abandoned, unwanted, and empty and one in which the future looked lonely and hopeless—a very depressed child.

Kristy's anger and aggression surfaced in her therapy sessions. Her favorite animal was a tiger. She chose tigers and lions in her play. Kristy said she had never been around a tiger, "but I've always wanted to have a pet tiger . . . I like dangerous animals."

Kristy related much better to men than to women. She liked her Uncle (adoptive father) Gary, and was cooperative with him. She had frequent conflicts with her Aunt (adoptive mother) Gwen and attachment to her fluctuated from cooperation to anger and rebellion. Kristy liked having a male therapist and identified with me. She included me as a partner in some of her storytelling.

In the first year of treatment, Kristy spoke of having suicidal thoughts and impulses. She said that, at age ten, she had taken "an overdose" of headache medicine.

Kristy admitted that she still had periodic impulses now to hurt herself. She made a verbal contract with me not to act on any suicidal impulse and to call me/tell me when such thoughts and impulses were present.

During the rest of the first year and one-half of treatment, aggression and separation themes were a frequent focus in therapy. Mild progress continued. There were several months in which depression symptoms were mild, and family and school relationships improved.

Serious problems occurred with the onset of adolescence at age thirteen. After a five-month absence, Gary and Gwen brought Kristy back for therapy. Their concerns were:

1. Sexually provocative language and sexual advances to boys on the school bus and to her brother's teenage friend.
2. Lying and deceptive behavior at home.
3. Stealing some of Gwen's jewelry.

Again, Kristy responded to individual therapy and family therapy with improvement in behavior problems. She said, "I don't know why I said all that sexual language." She accepted her parents' restrictions with minimal resentment. She went to summer church camp and returned saying, "I've changed since I went to camp."

Her Uncle Gary confirmed that her behavior and attitude had changed. Behavior problems were addressed at home and in therapy and stayed at manageable levels the rest of her thirteenth year.

At age fourteen, Kristy had moved from a shy, withdrawn, and depressed child to an expressive and assertive teenager. Her sexual desires were strong; she became obsessed with a sixteen-year-old student. Kristy described herself as "I'm crazy at school. I do crazy things. I go up to people and tell them what I think. I shock them, make them laugh." Kristy enjoyed this adolescent identity.

During the year, Kristy made two suicidal gestures. She scratched her face with a razor blade, and then she put a plastic bag in her bed and told Aunt Gwen that she intended to suffocate herself. Kristy had intense mood swings from excitement and elation to anger and a depressed mood. Treatment focused on her moods and behavior. Again, problems improved. Kristy began the ninth grade excited about school with a typical adolescent interest in boys. Therapy was discontinued for a year by her parents after Kristy's mild improvement.

I saw Kristy and her Uncle Gary when she was fifteen and enrolled in the tenth grade. She was sexually active and very depressed. She had been raped ten days earlier when she went with a male acquaintance of a few hours to a house where strangers were present. Kristy blamed herself, saying, "It's my fault for going to that house. Something is wrong with me." Her school grades dropped, she had run away from home one month earlier and was drinking alcoholic beverages to excess. Kristy was dressed in black, kept her face covered by her long hair, wore no makeup in contrast to her previous grooming, and was anxious and perspiring. She was in a very disturbed state.

Therapy ended at this time because the family's health insurance changed and Kristy was to be seen by a therapist covered by a managed-care company.

One year later at her parents' request, when Kristy was sixteen, I released her records to a residential treatment facility. I did a follow up phone call two months later. Kristy had been in residential care for two months, and was now back at home attending public school.

Kristy's case is an example of long-term treatment of a conduct disorder with adolescent onset, and dysthymia. It was a difficult case. Play therapy was useful as part of a multimodal treatment that included family therapy and behavior therapy, but gains were difficult and slow. I do not consider this a successful case. I wonder how Kristy fared in late adolescence. I have learned from conduct disorder cases to give my best effort.

It is often not enough.

PRACTICAL EXERCISE

Using a multimodal approach, develop treatment plans for children with behavior problems.

1. Select a case with a diagnosis of Adjustment Disorder with Disturbance of Conduct.

   Description of Child:

   Specific Problems:

   Treatment Plans:

   Progress and Comments:

2. Select a case with diagnosis of Oppositional Defiant Disorder.

   Description of Child:

   Specific Problems:

   Treatment Plans:

   Progress and Comments:

3. Select a case with diagnosis of Attention Deficit Hyperactivity Disorder (ADHD).
   Description of Child:

   Specific Problems:

   Treatment Plans:

   Progress and Comments:

4. Select a case with a diagnosis of Conduct Disorder.
   Description of Child:

   Specific Problems:

   Treatment Plans:

   Progress and Comments:

CHILDQUOTE

A Forever Family

Five-year-old Darin had been in and out of foster care. When Mr. and Mrs. Brown, prospective adoptive parents, told him they would like for him to live with them, Darin stopped his playing, looked them directly in the eye and said, "Will you be my forever family?" The Browns adopted Darin. One year later they had an Adoption Birthday party for Darin. Afterwards Darin asked his adoptive mother, "Mom, forever is longer than a year, isn't it?."

More Understanding; Less Advice

Nine-year-old Stanton was struggling with a difficult visitation he had just had with his mother, the non-custodial parent. A gifted child, Stanton used most of the session to tell his therapist his problems with a parent who made lots of demands on him and was often angry at him. The therapist began to give Stanton some advice on how to cope, to try and make the best of the situation. Stanton interrupted the therapist with, "Well, thank you Mary Poppins. Just a spoon full of sugar makes the medicine go down. Is that what you mean?"

9

PLAY THERAPY APPLIED TO SEPARATION AND LOSS

Divorce, Absentee Parent, Death, Adoption, Foster Care

Play is a powerful stress management technique for children and for adults.

When we adults become overstressed, we look for time to get away: A vacation trip, or a day off for a favorite play activity such as fishing, skiing, shopping, reading, or entertainment. When children are faced with environmental stressors, they need and desire extra play time in their efforts to cope.

Play therapy is an integral part of a multimodal approach in the treatment of children who experience separation and loss, including divorce, an absentee parent, death of a family member, or the adjustments to a changing home environment of blended family, adoption, or foster care.

TYPICAL TREATMENT PLAN

1. Play therapy focused on the particular stressor(s), i.e., divorce, death.
2. Family therapy/consultation with the child's caregivers (parents, stepparents, grandparents, foster parents).
3. Referral to/consultation with community resources (school, support groups, governmental agencies, religious, and charitable organizations).
4. Bibliotherapy. Recommendation of information and self-help books on specific topics.

GUIDELINES FOR TREATING STRESSED CHILDREN

1. **High need for security.** The child's daily life has changed. Life has become unpredictable and scary. A basic question is, "Who will take care of me?" The child needs at least one adult on whom she can count to be there for her.
2. **The need for routine and sameness.** If stress has made life unpredictable and scary, there is comfort in having a routine. I encourage caregivers to provide such a boring, predictable routine that the child won't have to worry about what will hap-

pen next. Such sameness reduces anxiety and frees the child to use his energy for learning and loving.

3. **Time for healing.** Children grieve similarly and differently from adults. Children experience the phases of grief that are similar to adults: Shock and Denial, Anxiety, Anger, Sadness/Depression and Acceptance. But, children grieve differently, too: They move quickly back and forth from one stage to another. Children grieve in bits and pieces. A child may talk about her pain for a few minutes, then quickly change the subject and go play. A child can only deal with so much pain at one time. A child experiences stress developmentally: At her cognitive and emotional level, a five-year-old child who loses a family member grieves at a young child's level, and is likely to have grief issues when she is an older child or adolescent as well. The child needs to have therapy available at different ages.

4. **Grief therapy.** We may tend to avoid painful issues with our child because of our own discomfort. The child needs the therapist to model genuineness, empathy, directness and sensitivity. She needs to be treated as normally as possible. Most children have significant coping strength. I want to create a safe therapeutic environment in which the child draws on her coping ability and I provide direction so that healing can occur.

5. **Help the parent/caregiver help the child.** "How can I help my child?" is a parent's common concern. Parents need to be involved in the child's

therapy. In joint sessions and parent consultation the therapist can provide guidance and specific recommendations to the parent.

When a parent/caregiver is distraught, depressed or emotionally overwhelmed, the child is likely to become anxious, insecure, demanding of more attention and/or more difficult to manage. The parents may need referral for individual therapy or a support group. I tell parents that getting support for themselves is an important way to help their child.

DIVORCE

Case Example One—Harold, Ten-Year-Old Boy Facing His Parents' Divorce

This case is an example of the difficulty in treating a child when one parent refuses to be involved in the child's treatment.

Harold was brought to therapy by his stressed mother, Mrs. Downs. Presenting problems included stress-induced asthma that resulted in school absences sixty percent of the previous month, initial divorce proceedings after long-term marital problems, and Harold's overly dependent/resistive behavior toward his mother.

Harold's father was dominating and verbally abusive to his mother and now Harold was imitating some of this behavior. Harold was hungry for acceptance and time with his father, an outdoorsman and horse trainer. He rejected his son who was often sick from allergy and asthma attacks by calling him a "wimp" and other critical names.

The father avoided spending time with him and was often away from home. Harold didn't know when or how often he would see his father. Harold was initially resistive to therapy. He was uncomfortable talking about his health and family problems.

Treatment included behavior therapy for Harold's asthma and school avoidance, play therapy for divorce issues, and parent consultation and parent counseling for Harold's mother. His father was unwilling to participate in his son's therapy.

With such a child, it's important to find the techniques that work best for him.

Drawing and therapeutic storytelling were effective with Harold: Talk therapy was not.

In his second session, Harold drew a picture and told a story that expressed his concerns. He drew a barn that caught on fire. His story was: "This is a barn with horses in it. The barn caught on fire and someone came to get the horses out. The owner was gone."

I interpreted the "barn" to represent Harold's home, the "fire" his family's emotional distress of parent conflicts and pending physical separation. The "owner" I interpreted to be his absentee and emotionally unavailable father, and "someone" as the need for help for himself and his mother. This indicated that Harold was willing to accept therapeutic help "to get the horses out."

In this brief story, Harold expressed his fear and anger regarding the loss of his family and home, and his Dad's rejection of himself and his mother. Harold knew that soon the house, acreage and family horses would be sold and he would have to move. He was losing his father and his house.

In later drawings and storytelling, Harold's themes showed a desire for strength and power. He was interested in bicycle racing. His story was about how his hero gained courage in racing. I interpreted this as Harold's wish to be strong rather than thin and sickly.

Progress was revealed in Harold's drawings and story themes: He drew pictures of horses with stories that expressed his anger at a father figure: Smaller horses resisting bigger horses. Later, Harold began to accept the reality of his parents' divorce. His school attendance improved and resistance to his mother decreased. His drawings and stories included horses moving to a different barn that had plenty of hay and water.

Moderate progress was achieved through several months of individual therapy and consultation with Harold's mother. Regular consultation with his mother, Mrs. Downs, in addition to play therapy, was an important reason for Harold's progress. His mother was in significant distress due to emotional abuse and rejection by her husband. She was also exhausted from trying to help Harold with his overdependence on her, his health problems, and the frequent rejecting behavior from her son. In parent consultation, my goals were to provide supportive counseling for Mrs. Downs since she had a limited support system, to strengthen her parenting skills, and encourage her to be more assertive. Mrs. Downs was responsive. She set clearer limits with Harold and she acted more decisively in coping with the marriage dissolution.

Harold continued to have periodic depression due to the lack of a close relationship with his father and the unpredictability of visitation. But his asthma was manageable, his school attendance was regular and his relationship with his mother and peers improved.

Case Example Two—Philip, Five-Year-Old Boy, with Divorce, Visitation Problems, and a Blended Family

Philip's parents divorced when he was one-and-a-half years old. Both parents remarried. He lived with his mother and stepfather and had regular visitation for two years with his father and stepmother. During the previous year, there was a significant amount of anger between his parents that worsened and involved the courts for five months. For the past four months, Philip had behavior problems during visitation with his father including separation anxiety, anger behavior toward his father, physical aggression toward his two-year-old half-brother, and regression including daytime and nighttime enuresis (wetting).

Philip presented himself as a handsome child who expressed his thoughts and feelings and was active in play. In the initial session, Philip acknowledged that he got angry at his Dad's house and wanted to stay with his mother. At the second session, Philip remembered that the reason he was coming to see me was "To help my anger go away."

Philip is an example of treating a child adjusting to divorce, visitation, and blended family when both biological parents participate in therapy. Philip's parents alternated bringing him to therapy. Treatment consisted of consultation with both parents jointly and separately, and play therapy with parent involvement.

In the third session, Philip chose sand tray play. His behavior was impulsive and he expressed strong emotions. I introduced the theme of a horse that had to go to different homes. Philip resisted by making a "storm" in the sand. He built a sand castle, then "a tornado" destroyed it. In joint play, I introduced the theme of finding safe areas "For all the animals." Philip helped me build homes for the animals. He gave his moral of the story as "learning."

In the fourth session with Philip and his father, Philip said his anger was "Not big now . . . getting smaller." He had a successful weekend visit with his father without separation-from-mother anxiety. He even requested that his visit scheduled for one night be extended to two.

In the session with Philip and his Dad, I used bibliotherapy by reading *Dinosaur's Divorce* by Laurene Krasny Brown and Marc Brown (1986, Little, Brown and Company, Boston, New York, Toronto, London) to father and son. We discussed issues of visitation, stepfamilies and children's feelings about divorce. In sessions five, six and seven, Philip was eager for play time. He understood that "We talk first (about his anger and visitation problems), then play." Philip used play time to express his aggression im-

pulses and emotions, then responded to my therapeutic suggestions. In session five, in play with clay
and animals, I introduced the theme of a puppy dog
having "Two places to stay." Philip added dinosaurs
as a threat to the dog. He had a hero to protect the
dog and smaller animals, but ended the story with
dinosaurs destroying the play area. Aggression and
its control was still a core conflict for Philip and a
focus of my treatment.

In a joint session with his mother and individual
play therapy, Philip said his anger was "little." He
said, "Sometimes I can control myself; sometimes I
can't." Bedwetting and daytime enuresis stopped for
two months. Philip drew several pictures to express
some fears and aggression and his view of his parents. He drew a large flower and a little flower. The
large flower was motherly in that it protected the little
flower. Another drawing was of "A daddy long legs
spider that hurt a young spider." My story included a
"Baby spider that got help and the daddy spider
learned not to hurt the little spider and to be a safe
spider." Philip was afraid of his father's anger and
overly-serious actions. Dad was hurt and angry about
Philip's rejection of him and his acting-out behavior
during visitation prior to treatment.

In the seventh session of joint play with father
and son, both were relaxed and smiling. I gave them
a block-building assignment. The father was involved
and patient with his son. Philip was responsive to
joint play with Dad; his anger was "little" again.

On follow up visits, Philip's anger was manageable, visitation was satisfactory, and Philip's relation-

ship with his parents, stepparents, and stepsiblings was improved. Conflict between his parents was minimal.

ABSENTEE PARENT

The impact of an absentee parent upon his or her children can be enormous. I have seen many children longing for a call, visit, or contact from a parent that they see rarely, if at all. I have an adult friend who last saw his biological father when he was seven years old. He recalls that throughout childhood and adolescence, when he saw a strange car in the driveway, he immediately thought and wished that this might be his father coming to visit him and bring him a present.

The child tends to act out his hurt and anger at the absentee parent, often directing it toward the custodial parent who is present, sometimes internalizing it with depression and self-criticism, and sometimes with behavior problems at school and with peers.

Case Example Three—Carson, Ten-Year-Old Boy with Depression, ADHD, and an Absentee Father

Carson lived with his mother and eight-year-old sister. His parents had been divorced for four years. His father lived a thousand miles away; he visited once a year. There was almost no contact by phone or mail; just the yearly visit.

I treated Carson for one-and-a-half years. He had periodic anger outbursts in which he became self destructive. Early in treatment, he commented that he wanted "To kill myself." His self-esteem was low. Carson was easily upset when he didn't do well on a school assignment and would comment, "I'm stupid; I'm dumb."

Carson was reluctant to talk specifically about the pain of having an absentee father. I observed Carson before and after the yearly visit from his dad. For several weeks after such a visit, Carson was happier, more relaxed and had fewer behavior problems at school and home. He showed me presents "My dad bought me," and spoke of "Everything going good." The elation decreased by the second month, but the impact of a single visit had an amazing effect upon this lonely boy.

In play therapy, Carson often chose building projects with building blocks, sand tray, or clay. He responded positively to the attention I gave when observing his work, assisting when he needed help, and praising his effort. Carson gave me the role of a father figure. He was generally cooperative and made significant progress after four months of treatment. Carson made no suicidal threats in three months; depressive statements were less frequent and of lower intensity. At the beginning of treatment, his school was ready to place Carson in a class for the severely emotionally disturbed (SED) due to weekly disruptive outbursts of crying, throwing his books, hitting himself, and threatening to kill himself.

Carson was able to complete the remainder of the school year in a regular classroom. He continued to have periodic emotional reactions to mild frustrations but these were less intense than previously and occurred only two or three times each month.

The reasons for his improvement seemed related to having a father figure in therapy, weekly monitoring of his positive and negative school behavior, and concern and support expressed by his mother in family sessions. Play therapy gave him opportunities to release strong emotions that he could not articulate with words.

I gave Carson a limited choice in deciding what he wanted to play. Relational therapy issues were important to him. Having a father figure who was present and showed interest in him was powerful for Carson. Relating to Carson this way was more effective than talk therapy that focused on getting him to talk about his depression and loneliness. In forty-five-minute sessions I usually spent fifteen minutes jointly with Carson and his mother focusing on his home and school behavior, then thirty minutes in play therapy focusing on his projects. Carson's self esteem was bolstered through the pride and recognition he received for his building projects in therapy. Carson was talented in building. He responded to my attention and praise for his efforts. Carson began to smile and show pride in his work. He wanted his mother to see what he had made each session. Carson brought projects from home for me to see such as drawings, and vehicles constructed from Legos.

He had a male teacher the next school year and related well to him. His school adjustment improved and Carson's depression moved from moderate to mild severity. A primary reason for school progress in grades and behavior was having a male teacher with whom Carson formed an attachment.

Case Example Four—Sharon, Adjustment Disorder with Anxiety and Depression

Sharon was brought to me for therapy because of her distress about the lack of contact with her father who had moved out of state since the parents' divorce two years earlier. Her father had serious health problems. He called on rare occasions, but did not visit or call Sharon and her four-year-old brother on any regular basis.

Sharon was a bright, articulate six-year-old who spoke openly of her fears, sad feelings, and anger toward her father. Sharon worried about her father and was very concerned as to why he didn't show more interest in seeing her.

Play therapy techniques were effective with Sharon. She drew pictures, played with clay and animals, and participated in puppet play. Sharon expressed some of her worry and hurt. She drew a family picture that included her Dad; her story included him as part of the family. She expressed worry about whether he was healthy or becoming ill.

Sharon responded well to therapy and made moderate improvement during eight sessions over a five-month period. She had a strong personality, good social skills, and strong support from her mother. She was able to talk about her sadness and worry. Sharon agreed with my comment, "Your dad is missing out on seeing a neat daughter." The permanent absence of her father in her life caused major pain for this young daughter. But she coped by openly expressing her pain and by accepting support from family and friends.

DEATH OF A FAMILY MEMBER

Grieving children use play therapy to express their pain and sorrow over the loss of a parent or sibling. My main goals in treating such children are to facilitate healthy grieving and to provide support and direction for caregivers.

Case Example Five—Becky, Six-Year-Old Girl Coping with the Sudden Death of Her Mother

Becky's case is also an example in Chapters 2 and 4. She was referred to me for grief reactions to the sudden death of her mother caused by a brain aneurysm. Her family had also experienced the death of seven other relatives during the past three years.

Grief therapy with Becky focused on her very high needs for security and emotional support, and for grief therapy and support for her depressed father. I saw Becky over a three-year period. The first year I saw her and her father two to four times per month. The second year, I saw her one to two times each month. The third year consisted of monthly sessions regarding adjustment to her father's remarriage and to her blended family.

In initial treatment, Becky fluctuated from a

strong, assertive child to regressed dependency. Nighttime fears and separation anxiety were prominent at home although Becky also tried to assume the role of "Daddy's helper."

In play therapy, Becky liked to draw pictures, and play with the dollhouse and puppets. She liked to role play with me; she sometimes took the role of teacher and other times the role of the small child. Anxiety was the prominent emotion the first months of treatment; she also experienced short periods of depression. She would talk only briefly about her deceased mother. The pain was too great for any prolonged discussion. This is a typical reaction of grieving children.

Becky had difficulty accepting the time limits of a therapy session. Her needs were so great that she usually left a session wanting more time. Her daily schedule of school and day care with relatives, due to her father's work schedule, was stressful. Her father complained that Becky "dawdled" in the mornings when he was trying to get her ready to leave the house.

Hurrying was stressful to Becky. She expressed her severe grief by resisting transitions, particularly going to school in the mornings and leaving the therapist's office at the end of sessions.

In the seventh session, Becky expressed anger at her deceased mother for not being there "So I could give her a Valentine." In this and subsequent holiday periods, Becky expressed anger and sadness over it "Not being fair" that she didn't have a mother to share holidays. At age six-and-a-half, she struggled with the reality of the permanence of death. With her extended family and in most of our therapy sessions, Becky presented herself as a happy, active child. At home with her father, she exhibited fear, anger, and sadness. She began to express more grief in subsequent play therapy sessions.

In the eighth session, using animal puppet play, I focused on the little sheep coping with fears when the mother sheep was absent. Becky accepted my focus on parent absence and took her typical assertive role in which she was the "doctor" who helped the little sheep. She continued this theme in the next session in which she took the role of "older sister" taking care of the little brother who had no parents. By taking the caregiver role, Becky met her needs to have some control of stressful situations and to express the hurting child who desperately needed nurturing and care.

In the twelfth session, Becky was able to be more focused in her grief. In puppet play, she asked for the therapist's help when I introduced the theme of a baby elephant coping with the loss of its mother. In the next session, Becky's dad reported that, at home, Becky had been talking about her mother more frequently and that, for the first time, Becky had told her classmates that her mother had died.

I used bibliotherapy on several occasions with Becky. I read to her the Sesame Street book *I'll Miss You, Mr. Hooper* based on the television script by Norman Stiles (1984, Random House/Children's Television Workshop, New York and Canada). This helped Becky to talk more about her grief.

Becky was responsive to mutual storytelling with the use of audio recordings of her story. She usually wanted her dad to listen to her recorded stories. Frequent themes were separation fears, coping with the death of her mother, and available support.

Becky became more direct in expressing her fears and sadness. She said, "I miss my mother a lot . . . I still feel sad . . . I talk to my teacher and my dad about Mommy."

After nine months of treatment, Becky was faced with her dad's dating and the possibility of having a stepmother. Becky's responses were typical for her. On one hand, she was excited and involved in having contact with a mother figure and her three children. On the other hand, she became more possessive of her father's time and attention. Becky did voice concern that her dad "Might give me to someone else and marry Jan (a potential stepmother) and her kids." I used joint sessions with Becky and her father to focus on Becky's concerns and family changes. Becky was vulnerable at this time. On the week that her great-grandfather died, Becky was tearful. She told me, "I'm afraid Daddy will leave and never come back; he might die like Mommy." Becky's mother had gone to work one day, had an aneurysm, and when Becky saw her at the hospital, she had already died. It was Halloween time. Becky insisted that her Halloween pumpkin be "A crying pumpkin."

After the first year of therapy, Becky grieved more openly and talked with her father about her concerns. When her father broke up with Jan, Becky said, "I hoped she would be my mother . . . it's not fair that I don't have a mother." Her insecurity was strong. She often held her mother's picture and carried the stuffed animal given by her mother. In one session around Christmastime, Becky said, "It's hard during the holidays for Daddy and me." Referring to her father's periodic irritability, Becky said, "Parents get mad sometimes, but they still love you." Becky's father was concerned that his emotional state had a detrimental effect on Becky. He continued with parent consultation as needed. Regular therapy and parent consultation were still a significant part of Becky's treatment.

In a subsequent session, Becky displayed significant insight and coping strength. She was verbal about missing her mother around Christmastime. She was sad that "Mommy will not come back, but we can see her when we die." She spoke of how important her mother would always be to her. "I keep a picture of her by my bed." Becky expressed hope that someday "My Dad and me will find a nice lady." Becky was able to verbalize her sadness to me and to her father. She concluded her mutual storytelling with me with the theme of "Being friends, forever and ever and ever."

Becky was able to speak about "Missing my Mommy still." She said, "I didn't get to tell her goodbye" (before she died). "The hardest part was when Daddy told me Mommy had died. " A day care child had told Becky her mother had died before her father told her. "I thought Mommy was just sick in the hospital, that she fainted. I didn't know she had died." After she expressed her grief in a five-minute talk, Becky moved to creative play.

Frequent play therapy themes thereafter were about puppets moving and saying goodbye, "Going away parties," positive reuniting with friends, continued sadness of "missing my Mommy."

After a year and a half, I saw Becky once a month. Her father remarried. Therapy focused on establishing a relationship with her stepmother, Pat, and Becky's concerns about changes in her family.

Becky's role changed from "Dad's helper," in which she often took the role of an older child. Moving from her house was a big adjustment. Becky expressed some sadness and fear. "I've never moved before; my mother really liked that house."

As the time came to move from her old house to her blended family's new house, Becky became very concerned as to how the future owners might treat the old house and "Not take good care of it." In an animal puppet play session, I introduced the theme of moving to a new house. Becky quickly picked up this theme and we had a "Moving party."

The last eight months of treatment focused on Becky's adjustment to the blended family: It included individual and family sessions, and long-term grief issues. Becky began to accept the role of being a child rather than "Dad's helper." She performed well academically in school and had only mild behavior problems of "Talking too much" rather than doing the class assignment.

One day, Becky drew me a picture of Disneyland. It depicted a trip with her mother and father when she was four-and-a-half years old. The theme was memory of a happy time with her biological mother.

When therapy ended after three years, Becky was coping reasonably well with her blended family; her behavior and emotional problems were manageable. I thank Becky and her dad for letting me share as they coped with the devastating loss of a mother and a wife.

Case Example Six—Brad, Seven-Year-Old Boy Coping with the Sudden Death of his Father

Brad and his eleven-year-old brother, Charles, were referred to me by another therapist for grief therapy four months after the sudden death of their father. He died of a heart attack while on an out-of-town trip. Presenting problems included anger, anxiety, and sadness. Treatment consisted of twice-per-month individual sessions along with parent consultation. After one year, I saw them once a month for six months.

In the first appointment, Brad was sociable, outgoing, assertive, and very verbal. He was active in the session and eagerly participated in play. Brad's behavior was in contrast to that of his older brother, Charles, who was initially shy, quiet, and sad. The boys reacted differently to the traumatic death of their father based on their different personalities.

Brad's mother said her son had a personality similar to his deceased father. Brad had been told by family and friends, "You're just like your dad." Both father and son tended to be "Expansive, impulsive, dramatic, and sociable."

The primary grief reaction Brad experienced was anger. In school, he expressed anger at a classmate "For having a dad and I don't." He was angry at his father's business partners "For taking my dad's business away from us." Brad attempted to take the place of his father. He tried to be strong and powerful. Brad threatened to fight any adults who did not treat his family "right." He was angry that his father's office was rearranged.

In therapy sessions, Brad took a macho role. In contrast, at home he was very anxious at night, afraid to sleep alone "'Cause that's when I think of my Dad the most." Brad responded positively to individual therapy and formed an attachment to me. Brad preferred action tasks such as building block projects, sand tray play, and mutual storytelling activities. He followed my suggestions and interpretations in joint play and storytelling, usually in the latter part of a session after he expressed his mood in a "take charge" manner. Brad's need for some control over his life and his pain over the loss of his beloved father were strong.

In subsequent sessions, Brad acknowledged his sadness and depression. His ego state was fragile. He fluctuated from an angry, assertive child who tried to be strong, who expressed anger and resistance to teacher and mother, to the frightened and sad young boy who clung to his mother at home and reached out for adult nurturing. He so wanted his family to be complete again. Brad quickly identified with a male friend of his mother and asked him, "When are you going to marry my mother?"

Brad sometimes turned his anger inward and engaged in self-punishment. "Sometimes when I'm angry, I hit myself on the head like this."

Brad responded well to play therapy with play animals and a miniature house.

I introduced the theme of a pet lion whose home was damaged and the lion's lashing out in anger. Together, Brad and I rebuilt the lion's house, adding a room and including many other animals. The pet lion was chosen because of Brad's need for power and strength. The damaged home represented the death of Brad's father. The added room was a means of rebuilding the family. The additional animals were an expression of Brad's desire and need for social support from family and friends.

In one of the house and lion sessions, I had the lion run away in anger. Brad corrected me by saying the lion "Wasn't angry; he was just going to his Dad's grave." He was then able to talk more about his sadness.

Brad coped well for two months, but he and his brother, Charles, had a difficult time as the holiday season and the first-year anniversary of their father's death approached. Brad expressed significant anger at school and home during this period. In therapy sessions, he chose aggressive themes of fighting. He avoided acknowledging or talking about his pain, but acted it out in therapy and in his environment. Serious depression symptoms were expressed, especially at the first anniversary. Brad said he would like to die so he "could see my dad in heaven."

In this session, I used audio-taped storytelling in which I told this story: "A storm came and hit this village and hurt the people. The people were sad and frightened. After that, they were afraid another storm would come to their village."

In response to my story, Brad chose sand tray play. He built a road and repeated the storm theme in which he buried people and vehicles. Brad made a tomb for the people. At the end of his story, he changed the tomb to a cave. "The boy and his mom were recovered."

Brad played this tape for his mother in joint session time. Mother and son then talked about the day his dad died, how his mother was called to an out-of-town hospital, not knowing whether her husband was already dead. Brad expressed his wish that he had gone to the hospital with his mother and seen his dad's body. It was an intimate, sharing-of-pain time for mother and son.

In his next session, Brad and I built a monument in the sand in honor of his father. Brad wrote his dad's name in the sand and put pet dogs there: "My dad liked dogs." I told this story about "Monument Land" as a follow up.

"Once upon a time a family lost its dad. They had a ranch. They wanted to remember Dad always so they changed the name of the ranch to Monument Land. The boys built a hill and wrote Dad's name on the top. They decorated the hill with statues of dogs 'cause Dad loved dogs. They added special things like a barn for his favorite horse to remember Dad. It was a fine Monument Land." (This part of the story was to encourage building a scrapbook of good memories about Brad's father.)

"After a while, one brother came up with an idea. He said, 'I like Monument Land but now let's live on the land and build things that our Dad taught us.' So that's what they decided. They smoothed the land and built a house for the people and a barn for the animals. They planted crops and grew food for everyone. They built a lake for swimming. They had a forest for exploring and hunting. They changed the name of their ranch from Monument Land to Living Land."

My thinking in this story was to encourage Brad to always remember his father. But I also wanted Brad to look to the future and live as his father's son—to grow and develop—not just look backward in grief and sadness. Brad was responsive to the story.

Brad's grief reactions decreased and he moved to the acceptance and rebuilding stages of grief with fewer periods of sadness. This was a critical time in Brad's and his family's grief experience. He shared some of his pain and accepted my involvement and suggestions. Brad's mother was sensitive to and daily involved in Brad's care. She was very nurturing to her son.

After nine months of treatment, Brad's depression and anger were significantly decreased. He continued to have mood swings and occasional periods of behavior problems of resistiveness to his mother and school. But his school achievement was good. Brad's expressive, dramatic, and assertive personality traits were evident.

In one session, Brad chose blocks to "rebuild a house." He took extra time to make the house strong. He built a protective metal guard around the house and built a safety fence around the children's room. I interpreted this as a positive sign regarding grief adjustment, but with continued fears. Brad's mother reported the primary grief symptom as being night-time fears.

Brad was seen as needed during the last six months of treatment. He responded to continued therapy with active play themes. He moved to the developmental levels of chance and skill games. There were times of regression, especially at holidays and at the beginning of the school year. He tested limits with his mother at times and resisted doing his school work, but responded positively when his mother set limits. I used behavior therapy techniques with Brad to decrease his nighttime fears. He slept in his own room all but three nights in eight weeks. Brad said he still thought of his dad at night, but he had faced his fears and they were overcome.

Grief over the loss of a parent is long-term. A child like Brad usually needs at least one year of therapy, with additional treatment at other times during childhood.

Case Example Seven—Shelly, Three-and-a-Half Year-Old Girl, Death Of Two Siblings

Shelly was a beautiful little girl with black hair and dark brown eyes. She had good social skills and was able to reach out to adults. After a few sessions, Shelly would check in with my secretary, "I sure do need to see Dr. Price." Who could not have been attracted to this charming child?

I saw Shelly and her mother for grief therapy due to the tragic death of her two sisters, ages six and eight, in a traffic accident. Shelly's presenting problems were extreme fears of traveling in a car, fears of separation from her mother, and sadness. The mother was usually present at the sessions that included individual play therapy, joint play therapy with Shelly and her mother, and parent counseling. The treatment lasted for one year.

Shelly had experienced the trauma of being injured in the same car accident that killed her two sisters. She had vivid memories of being in the car after the accident and of the emergency vehicles at the scene. Treatment of her trauma was the first step. Shelly was very frightened when she heard police or ambulance sirens. She was afraid to be away from her mother and her mother was frightened to be away from Shelly for any time.

I encouraged the mother to continue in individual therapy with her counselor. I recommended desensitization steps for fear of traveling in a car and for mother-daughter separation fears. This remarkably courageous little girl responded well to treatment. She was able to ride in a car with her mother and stepfather with mild discomfort within three months. Shelly had the support of her extended family and was able to go for short visits to her grandparents. She accepted being separated from her mother for one to two hours when her stepfather or grandparents cared for her.

Shelly quickly established a routine in therapy that she repeated at the beginning of each session. She preferred the sand tray with animals and small dolls. She spent parts of several sessions burying the animals and people in the sand. This behavior is not uncommon with young children who act out a death by repeatedly burying animals and objects.

In one session, Shelly had her mother help her make favorite animals from clay that represented her two sisters. Shelly spoke of her deceased sisters, and included them in some of her play. Shelly was described by her mother as dependent on her two older sisters who hovered over her. She was shy and relied on them to communicate many of her desires. Since their death, Shelly's assertive and independent traits had surfaced, to her mother's surprise. In therapy, Shelly often took the lead role in play, was verbal in expressing her desires, and often acted independently. Shelly's inner strengths were seen in how she coped with such trauma and how she was able to respond to grief therapy.

Shelly was able to verbalize her anger and sadness over the car accident and to seek out and accept emotional support from family and therapist. She expressed her grief with her mother, sometimes verbally and often with her actions. She used play therapy and play at home to express her pain, and as a means of coping with such extreme stressors. The major way in which she dealt with separation fears was by separating herself in independent play. Shelly was able to engage in play for one or more hours at home with her mother's limited supervision.

At the end of one year, Shelly was coming for treatment once a month and was coping remarkably well. Treatment was discontinued by her mother. Shelly is likely to need additional therapy through childhood and adolescence as she moves through future developmental stages.

ADOPTION

Children who are adopted, even in infancy, often need family and individual counseling and guidance regarding possible issues of:

- The child's biological history and at-risk factors for medical, learning, behavioral, and emotional problems.
- The child's need to know information about his biological parents and the parents' concerns about how much to share with their child, and when to share it.
- The parents' difficulty in parenting an adopted child whose temperament is quite different from their own.
- The child's self-concept of being an adopted child and how the child is perceived and treated by peers.
- The older child's previous history regarding bonding during infancy, attachment to adults, possible neglect and/or abuse; the child's present ability to form an attachment to adoptive parents.
- The child's sense of abandonment by biological parents and fear of abandonment by adoptive parents and significant others.
- The adolescent's desire to contact biological parents and adoptive parents' concerns and fears regarding such contact.

Adam, in Chapter 8, is an example of a child whose temperament was very different from his religious family. His behavior problems were difficult for his adoptive parents to comprehend. Adam also per-ceived himself as the different and difficult child.

His desire to know more about his biological parents was a significant issue. When his parents were willing to talk with him, listen to and answer his questions about adoption, Adam's emotional state and behavior improved.

FOSTER CARE

I have treated a significant number of children in both short-term and long-term foster care. Separation and loss and attachment issues are major issues with fos-ter children. Assessing for neglect and/or abuse is necessary.

A major goal in therapy with foster children is to provide an experience in which the child can form some attachment with an adult and have closure at the end of treatment in which the child and I are able to say goodbye. Sometimes we do this with a "party." I try to give the child two or three sessions for termi-nations. It is quite disturbing if the child's treatment is abruptly interrupted and he moves without time to say goodbye. This is one more unfinished separa-tion time. I try to work with case managers and fos-ter parents around a goal of closure.

Therapists who work with foster children need to be aware of attachment issues. Some children form "pseudo-attachments," in which the child may be very friendly and immediately attach to the thera-pist. Some foster children draw me a picture of "Dr. Price" in the first or second session with the words,

"I love you." This can be flattering to the therapist but genuine attachment takes time. The child who forms instant attachment is likely to exhibit masked anger and resentment both to the therapist and the foster parents. Her anger is more likely to be expressed in passive aggressive ways. Examples are: "forgetting" to do an assigned task, "accidents" in which child damages something important to family, stealing of mother's favorite jewelry, avoidance of a hug initiated by parent.

Some children avoid attachment and withdraw from or resist foster parents and teachers. Foster parents can easily get caught up in power struggles with the child. This conflict is one way the child protects himself from genuine attachment and intimacy. Foster children are usually fiercely loyal to their biological parent(s). Such caring needs to be accepted and discussed with the child, instead of focusing on how badly the parent(s) treated the child.

Deanna, whom I wrote about in Chapter 6, was in long-term foster care. I used her life story as a means for Deanna to express how important her biological mother was to her. The life story also was an effort for Deanna to tell her history that included all of her childhood—both pleasant and unpleasant.

Case Example Eight—Darin, Five-Year-Old Boy, Dealing with Foster Care and Adoption

Darin's presenting problems were multiple separations from his biological mother, a history of neglect and abuse, severe anxiety, hyperactivity, impulsive behavior.

When I first met Darin, he was in a repeat home placement with a single adult foster mother. Darin had been removed from his biological mother for the second time because she neglected and abused him, and was a drug user. Darin experienced severe behavior problems in day care and was difficult to manage even by his caring and skilled foster mother, Margaret.

In my office, Darin was anxious, impulsive and overactive. Anxiety was primary with aggressive play as a secondary symptom. He loved to play Ninja Turtles. He took the role of Leonardo and fought off enemies. I set boundaries requiring that he not hit people or property, but allowed Darin to act out his aggressive impulses. We spent part of several sessions "fighting the mean guys" and looking for them throughout my office.

Treatment lasted for one year. We used play therapy, behavior therapy for limit setting, consultation with foster mother Margaret for home and behavior problems, guidance in how to meet Darin's emotional needs, and consultation with his social worker.

Darin required sameness in every session for he repeated the play activity from previous sessions. It took him twenty to thirty minutes to calm down enough to respond to my directed play. Darin was impulsive and easily aroused. Anxiety was high. Any change or transition was anxiety-producing for Darin. He had difficulty with sessions ending. Several times when I told him, "Darin, we have five minutes left for today; I'll set the timer," Darin would react by jumping up and running out of the office.

Progress was slow. Two treatment goals were to reduce his anxiety-driven hyperactivity and to decrease his wild public behavior in day care and social situations. Darin began to make progress.

By establishing routine and sameness in therapy and at home, Darin's anxiety levels reduced from severe to moderate. Margaret's caring and persistence in keeping this difficult child was a major contributing factor. Being permitted opportunity to express his fears and aggressive impulses in play therapy seemed to help reduce aggressive play in day care. Teaching Darin impulse control through therapist-demonstrated breathing exercises and behavior rehearsal, introduced the concept that he could have some control over negative behavior. Play therapy games provided a safe setting with no external threats. This allowed Darin to form a relationship with his therapist and to have fun experiences of play, which Darin most needed. These all contributed to the slow but continuous progress in therapy.

Behavior problems were reduced in frequency and intensity. He responded to sameness and routine in his daily schedule, but minor changes still disturbed him. Darin became able to talk briefly with me and his foster mother about his biological mother, and some of her neglect and abuse. Darin's fear of abandonment was based on his family history and the multiple separations from his caregivers.

In one session, Darin demonstrated for me how to manage his anger. He was playing wildly as

Leonardo. I asked him to "Show the boys and girls how to control their anger." Darin stopped, thought for five seconds, took his warrior headband off, and put his pool stick "swords" down. He took cushions from the sofa and said, "You hit the pillows like this" as he pounded the pillow several times; then he put the cushions neatly back in place. I asked Darin how he could tell when he was angry. He said, "My tummy hurts." This was the best way he understood when he was unhappy. I was so pleased that he was able to exert such self-control over his behavior.

Darin then chose to play his favorite board game of *Candyland*. Darin's developmental level was usually at the Win level: He needed total control of the game with the therapist as observer. On this day, he took the Win-Win level in which both child and therapist were "winners." Darin turned all the *Candyland* cards face up so he could control the winner. When he got close to winning, he took my piece and made sure I got to *Candyland* at the same time he did. He ended by holding both his and my playing pieces and having them kiss each other. He felt safe, and was able to express affection to me in a safe manner.

My involvement in Darin's adoption was a special experience. After nine months of therapy, his social worker found a prospective family in a different town. Darin made three visits to them: One brief visit, in which he met the prospective parents, the Browns, with his foster mother present; a second visit over a weekend at the Brown's home with a return to foster care, and a final visit at the Brown's home for several days.

His social worker arranged with me to have all

interested parties meet in my office with Darin. I explained to him that the Browns wanted him to live with them and be their child. Darin was uncomfortable during some of the explanation. He began playing, then turned to Mr. and Mrs. Brown and said, "Will you be my forever family?"

Darin moved to the Brown's home. They were a loving family who had older biological children and one adopted child with physical handicaps. The Brown's were aware of Darin's mild developmental delays and need for some remedial instruction, along with therapy for his emotional problems. They brought him back to see me for three sessions and had a local therapist available for additional therapy as needed. Darin was able to see Margaret, his former foster mother, several times. She took the role of an "aunt," who was part of his family.

Mrs. Brown wrote me a letter one year later. She said that the family had a celebration for Darin's "Adoption Birthday." Darin was excited about the party. That evening in special time with his mother, Darin said, "Forever is more than a year, isn't it, Mom?" With so many home placement changes, Darin finally was able to think of his family as permanent. They became, indeed, his "forever family."

Case Example Nine—Gina, Eight-Year-Old Girl in Long-Term Foster Care, with a Developmental Disability and a Thought Disorder

I knew Gina from age eight until age eighteen. She was referred for therapy due to chronic neglect and abuse before foster care placement. She lived with one of the most special foster mothers I have ever known. Mrs. Fields never gave up on a child despite severe problems.

When I began treatment, Gina was a frightened, severely disturbed, attractive girl who was the classic example of learned helplessness. She sat with her head down, with body language similar to a whipped puppy. She did not know how to express herself and relied on adults for directions. Gina required special education for a mild mental handicap.

Therapy with Gina included relationship building, treatment for abuse, and consultation with foster parents, a special education teacher, and a social worker.

Gina made mild progress during one year of treatment. She was less frightened and responded to individual therapy in which she could talk about her problems and frustrations. Gina had a foster family that accepted her and included her in all family activities. She was in a class for multiple handicapped children for her poor gross and fine motor skills and her mental handicap. Gina's teacher was a positive influence.

Gina was placed in an adoptive home. Her adoptive parents were very involved in Gina's education and counseling. Her mother was determined to help Gina progress to as nearly normal as possible. But after four years of effort that included home schooling, Gina, at age thirteen was at second grade level academically and seriously lacking in social skills. She had difficulty with her peers. The adoptive parents now had two young biological daughters who had average abilities and were close to surpassing Gina in cognitive and adaptive functioning.

Gina's adoptive parents abruptly returned her to social services and relinquished all parental rights. Gina was reunited with Mrs. Fields for long-term foster care. I provided therapy for Gina at various periods for the next five years. Progress was difficult. Her treatment included school consultation, parent consultation, and supportive and directive therapy. Gina took the opportunity to talk about her depression and multiple rejections by biological and adoptive parents. She formed an attachment to me as a long-term authority figure. Mrs. Fields provided a good home for Gina and accepted her limitations.

The last time I saw Gina, she had finished special education high school but was unable to cope with work outside the home. She received medication management by her psychiatrist. Gina had become a permanent member of the Fields family and was attached to it. She was able to assist in housekeeping chores for the family.

Gina is an example of an emotionally and mentally handicapped child who needs long-term care and is unable to live on her own.

For another case example of foster care, see Sandra, age five, in Chapter 4.

PRACTICAL EXERCISE

Develop a treatment plan for a child with at least one of the following environmental stressors. Discuss the case with a colleague.

1. Divorce
   Description of Child:

   Specific Problem(s):

   Treatment Plans:

   Progress and Comments:

2. Absentee Parent
   Description of Child:

   Specific Problem(s):

   Treatment Plans:

   Progress and Comments:

3. Death of a family member
   Description of Child:

   Specific Problem(s):

   Treatment Plans:

   Progress and Comments:

4. Adoption
   Description of Child:

   Specific Problem(s):

   Treatment Plans:

   Progress and Comments:

5. Foster Care

   Description of Child:

   Specific Problem(s):

   Treatment Plans:

   Progress and Comments:

CHILDQUOTE

The Rewards I Need

Ten-year-old Rhonda was definite about the rewards she wanted to receive. At the end of a therapy session Rhonda told her therapist, "When you go out to the front (reception room), tell my Mom that what I really need is lots of love and a new computer game."

10

PLAY THERAPY APPLIED TO TRAUMA AND ILLNESS

Violence, Natural Disasters, Illness

VIOLENCE

In providing treatment to children, you are likely to see ones who are victims of various kinds of violence such as those who have witnessed the murder of a parent or sibling, domestic violence, an act of terrorism, neglect and abuse—physical, emotional, sexual—and car wrecks.

I have treated children who were traumatized by physical, sexual, and emotional abuse, extreme neglect, car wrecks, children who lost a parent or classmates in the Oklahoma City bombing, children who have been kidnapped, and a young child who witnessed the rape of her mother. I met with children in Bosnia who had witnessed firsthand the terror of war, the destruction of their homes, and the death of a parent.

How do we begin to treat such children? Begin with assessment and an accurate diagnosis. Important areas to assess:

- The severity of the stressor.
- The length of the trauma experienced: acute versus chronic.
- The support system available (parents, family members, friends, teachers, community resources).
- The child's coping ability: Resilient versus vulnerable.
- The child's symptoms.

Look for PTSD symptoms. Post-Traumatic Stress Disorder (PTSD) is a common diagnosis for such children. Symptoms found in PTSD children include:

- Nightmares.
- Preoccupation with traumatic event.
- Minimal ability to enjoy themselves in play and poor interactions with others.
- Difficulty to relax and enjoy themselves.
- Hyperarousal and hypervigilance.
- Numbing of affect.
- Vacillation between withdrawal, friendliness and

aggressive outbursts (compliant, withdrawn, aggressive).

- Fears.
- Avoidance behavior.
- Substance abuse.
- Acting out sexually.
- Among adolescents, guilt, and being secretive.
- Psychogenic amnesia, flashbacks and psychic numbing which are often seen in adult PTSD patients; less common among PTSD children.

Treatment Guidelines

- Provide an atmosphere for the child to express herself. The child needs a safe setting that encourages her to reveal hurts and concerns.
- Allow the child to form an attachment to you. A child who has been traumatized has a great need to be grounded; to be attached to another person.
- Help the child utilize all the emotional support available to him in his home, school and community.
- Address treatment issues through both symbolic play (clay and animals, puppets, drawings, storytelling) and, when appropriate, rehearsal play in which the child practices how to handle problems.
- Include caregivers in treatment through regular consultation, family therapy, participation in play therapy.

- With traumatized children particularly, focus on the present: How they feel now, learning how to cope, forming attachments to present caregivers.

For preschool and school age children, play is the primary method they use to express their trauma. Drawings with storytelling, clay modeling, and sand tray play, with therapeutic storytelling are particularly useful.

Case Example One—Shelly, Three-and-a-Half Year-Old Girl, Passenger in Fatal Car Collision

Shelly (described in Chapter 9) was a victim of road rage. She experienced the terror of a car chase, the impact of the crash, and the death of her two sisters who were passengers in the car. Shelly was injured, trapped in the car, and was conscious of events until emergency teams rescued her.

How can play therapy best be used with a traumatized child such as Shelly? Shelly responded to the sameness in my office setting, to opportunity to repeat trauma scenes with the sand tray, the dollhouse, and with clay and animals. I provided a safe atmosphere for Shelly, gave her freedom to choose the day's activity, and played with her—sometimes as an observer, sometimes as a participant. She formed an attachment to me. I set boundaries if and when needed to assure her that an adult would set limits and take charge when she felt out of control. As I observed Shelly's play themes, I introduced a story or activity that addressed her issues of the day: Fear, sadness, anger, insecurity, desire for mother's nurturing or her need for autonomy and control.

Initial treatment focused on the trauma of the car crash. Shelly preferred sand tray play. Early in treatment she was preoccupied with separation from her mother and severe fear reactions to ambulance and police car sirens, and the subject of death.

Symbolic play and rehearsal play were effective with Shelly. She had strong fear reactions when she heard a police car, ambulance or fire truck. To ride in a car or van after the accident was frightening. In her sand tray play, I introduced a toy ambulance, fire truck, and police car. Together we practiced playing with emergency vehicles, later using them to help injured people. I made siren sounds at the level Shelly could tolerate to desensitize her fears. Real life (in vivo) desensitization was part of her treatment. Shelly's mother and I developed a plan of riding in the car beginning with regular short rides with her parent or grandparent to pleasant, familiar places like the grocery store or to see a relative. Shelly took her favorite toys, stuffed animal and/or snack with her in the car for comforting and a pleasant experience. The distance and frequency of car trips were increased as Shelly's phobic reactions decreased. Within a month she was able to ride to another town to visit her grandparents whose home was a favorite of Shelly's.

Shelly used the sand tray to express her preoccupation with death. She would repeatedly bury animal and people figures in the sand stating that they died. Children under age five or six do not have the cognitive ability to understand death as permanent.

Shelly's preoccupation of burying and unburying play figures was her effort to cope with the reality of the death of her sisters.

Shelly had been very dependent upon her two older sisters before their deaths. At home and in therapy Shelly began to show her assertive side—wanting to tell her mother and me what she wanted to do, choosing independent play sometimes, expressing her thoughts without shyness and often being assertive. I reinforced these independent steps. Shelly's statements included, "Dr. Max, I need to see you today . . . I want to play with the playdough (clay). . . . Let's do it this way. . . . No, I don't want to do that." I interpreted her assertive play as a healthy sign. She was moving from helpless to an active stance.

In one session, Shelly's focus was on remembering her deceased sisters. We used clay to make animals that represented her family members. Shelly had her mother help her make two birds that she named Susie and Nicki (her sisters' names). One bird was blue, the other pink. Those were her sisters' favorite colors. Shelly played with the birds, had them take care of a smaller bird (Shelly), and later fly away. Remembering her sisters was the agenda of the day.

This session was followed by a family trip to the cemetery. Shelly and her mother took flowers to the graves. It was an emotional time, especially for her mother. For young Shelly it was a positive grieving and healing time. As in her therapy session, she was able to do something (bring flowers) for her sisters. It helped her understand death at her concrete level.

Shelly is an example of a brave young girl who

was faced with the tragic deaths of her sisters and her own injuries caused in a car crash.

Case Example Two—Billy, Seven-Year-Old Boy and Bobby, Four-Year-Old Boy, Death of Mother from Act of Terrorism

Billy was seven and Bobby was four years old when their mother was killed in the Oklahoma City bombing in 1995. They responded differently to the trauma.

Billy, the oldest, was presented with symptoms of anger, a drop in school performance, and a strong need to control. He was active in therapy: building projects, creating puppet shows for me and his father, and drawing pictures to express his hurt and concerns. He was comfortable acting out his grief but reluctant to talk about his pain.

Billy had built a fort in the back yard of his house. When the Murrah Federal Building was imploded after the search for bombing survivors and bodies of victims had ended, Billy went into the backyard and completely demolished his fort, expressing what the bombing had done to him and his home.

Billy was overly concerned about any changes in the family schedule. Billy needed some control over his environment after experiencing such trauma and loss. When his father and aunt planned a trip to the lake or to visit relatives, Billy insisted on packing all the suitcases and other trip items.

In contrast, four-year-old Bobby's main symptoms were anxiety and fear. He wanted to stay home with his aunt or his father. Bobby attended day care before his mother was killed, but now he was fearful of going to day care where he had been previously comfortable. He regressed to the two-to-three-year-old level, wanting to be cared for as a toddler. He cried frequently, especially at night, wanting his mother.

Bobby and Billy both responded to drawings, puppet play, and mutual storytelling in play therapy.

They had strong family support. An aunt moved to their house for several months to provide daily care. Bobby attached to her soon after his mother's death.

I saw him in treatment for four months. Separation anxiety and fears of going to day care lingered. The trauma of his mother's death for this four-year-old was severe. Bobby was able to cope in the safe confines of his home setting but continued to have fears away from the family. Bobby would need additional therapy periodically for the next one to two years.

Billy took the older child role of taking charge. At home, he helped with daily family chores and wanted to be involved in choices regarding family activities. Billy loved action including water sports of skiing and swimming. His anxiety was expressed in compulsive involvement in packing and planning for every family outing and trips.

Billy's emotional pain from the tragic loss of his mother was most evident in school behavior and achievement problems. He was a verbal and assertive child who had frequent arguments with his teacher and classmates, was easily frustrated with mild problems, and was often defensive about his actions. "I didn't do anything, he (classmate) just keeps bothering me . . . I don't like that dumb assignment; it was too hard."

In therapy sessions Billy took an active role. He liked to do puppet shows both jointly with therapist and by himself. With puppets, Billy would address his grief. One story was about the baby lamb who was lost and couldn't find his mother sheep ("Lambchop"). In a joint show, Billy acted out a monster puppet hurting timid puppets. He asked me to be a doctor puppet "to treat his hurts."

Billy profited from family and community support and from therapy, but he also continued to have periodic aggressive behavior problems and peer conflicts at school. He still had significant grief to resolve, particularly to move from grief stages of anxiety and anger to stages of sadness and acceptance. Billy would need continued grief therapy over the next two years.

Case Example Three—Andrea, Three-Year-Old, Death of Day Care Classmates

Andrea was a strong-willed young girl who had separation anxiety due to significant family stress prior to the Oklahoma City bombing. Andrea was absent from the day care center on the day of the bombing. Most of her classmates were killed that day.

Andrea's and her mother's reactions to this awful tragedy were understandable. Andrea experienced severe separation anxiety when away from her mother, had significant nighttime terrors, and periods of rage directed at her mother. Andrea's mother was terrified at how close she came to losing her daughter, and was in need of support and direction.

Play therapy with Andrea followed a predictable pattern. She quickly chose drawing and the dollhouse as her desired activities. Her drawings were remarkable for a three-year-old. She chose bright colors to make a picture for her mother. She chose somber colors to express her sadness and fears. Andrea formed an attachment with me. She liked the freedom of being in charge of her therapy activity. She liked me to observe her play and participate on occasion, but she usually preferred the Win stage of development activities—one in which she controlled her activity and I was there to watch and be available.

Play therapy and parent consultation were the primary treatment modalities used in Angela's treatment. I saw her for a year until she moved out of state. Her separation anxiety was reduced, but she was still subject to periodic episodes of severe anxiety and anger.

Case Example Four—Darin, Five-Year-Old Boy, Victim of Neglect and Abuse

Darin (in Chapter 9) is an example of a five-year-old victim of neglect, and physical and sexual abuse. He was an extremely anxious child. Play therapy provided a setting of order, security, limits and affection. He was able to use play therapy for some release of his fears and anger. See Chapter 9 for the description of his play therapy treatment and caregiver consultation.

Case Example Five—Gina, Eight-Year-Old Girl, Victim of Neglect and Abuse

Gina (in Chapter 9) is an example of a child who was a victim of chronic neglect and abuse. Gina had limited coping abilities; she functioned in the mild mental handicapped range. She relied on caregivers to protect and guide her, and never developed the social skills to make close friends.

Gina's abuse issues were addressed through conversation time in which she discussed her frustrations and fears. Gina formed a safe attachment with me while I taught her how to cope with peer relations by concrete role playing. Physical touch was not used with Gina due to her chronic abuse history. Symbolic touching, when I provided her with snacks, was effective. Gina was fortunate to have a long-term foster home that provided acceptance and a stable, secure family.

Case Example Six:—Bosnian Children, Victims of War

In the summer of 1996, I was privileged to visit a play therapy group in Central Bosnia. There were twelve children in the group aged six to nine years. All the children were refugees from their hometown that had been destroyed by the war. Nine of the children's fathers had been killed in the war. My son, Todd, is fluent in Bosnian and served as my interpreter.

I was impressed with the group's two leaders. Their materials were limited, but they used drawing effectively in leading the group. The children played active group games. The teachers set up an obstacle course in the room. As each child crawled through the space, encouraged by teachers and children, he received loud applause for successful completion. This was a self-esteem building activity.

The teacher shared the children's drawings with me. A common theme was each child's desire for peace. Several children drew pictures of airplanes dropping bombs on their village with the captions, "Stop the bombing," "Peace," "No more bombs."

A group leader did an effective job combining group storytelling with drawing. She used open-ended questions to involve the children. A sheet of drawing paper was taped to the wall. She drew a picture of a child in the woods with a neutral looking house in the middle of the woods. The teacher added to the drawing as the story progressed. The story began:

"Once there was a child walking through the woods and she came upon a house. What kind of house do you think it was?"

Several children volunteered their ideas about the house.

"Was is empty or occupied?"

The children decided it was occupied.

"Who was inside the house?"

The children decided a family lived in it.

The teacher added people inside the house. "Are the people kind or mean, sad, happy, or mad?"

The children used this time to express their curiosity and fears. Several children voiced the belief that the family was hostile. Others thought the family was friendly. In this story, children were faced with their reaction to a new situation. This was an effective way for the leader to help these war-traumatized children. They gave reactions to a new situation by means of a story which provided emotional distancing from their real life and was easier to talk about without being flooded by fears and sadness.

The consensus was that the family was sad. The teacher added sad facial features. "What did the child do? Run away? Stay where he was? Go to the house?"

A lively and spirited group discussion followed. The consensus was that the child was too frightened to go to the house but wanted to knock on the door because she was tired and hungry.

"How can we help the child not be so afraid?" the teacher asked. The children and teacher decided to add adults to be with the child. The teacher added two adults with one on each side of the child.

The group storytelling and drawing continued with the visiting family knocking on the door, asking to work for food and chopping wood for the fire. The owners cooked food in the fireplace and both families ate a meal in a warm house.

The teacher reviewed the drawings which were in sequence and retold the story that she and the group had created. I viewed this as a valuable storytelling experience. The story was drawn giving children a visual to focus their attention. The story was open ended in that children's present thoughts, feelings and attitudes were the substance of the story. The leaders guided the story to a problem solving finish.

Bosnian culture emphasizes the group; the community. Having the children do a group storytelling was fitting for Bosnian children.

Drawings and storytelling were effective techniques for these Bosnian children traumatized by war. They are also effective for children who have experienced other kinds of violence.

NATURAL DISASTERS (STORMS, FIRE, FLOODS)

The American Red Cross has prepared a pamphlet "Helping Children Cope with Disaster" (Federal Emergency Management Agency, ARC 4499, September, 1992) that includes material on children's response to disaster, advice to parents, and time for recovery. It notes that after a disaster, children are most afraid that:

- The event will happen again.
- Someone will be injured or killed.
- The child will be separated from the family.
- The child will be left alone.

CHILDRENS' COMMON REACTIONS FOLLOWING A DISASTER

- Be upset at the loss of a favorite toy, blanket, teddy bear, etc.

- Be angry. They may hit, throw, kick, and the like to show their anger.
- Become more active and restless.
- Be afraid of the disaster recurring. They may ask many times, "Will it happen again?"
- Worry about where they will live and what will happen to them.
- Be afraid to be left alone or afraid to sleep alone. The child may want to sleep with a parent or another person. Nightmares may occur.
- Regress to the behavior of a younger child. They may start sucking their thumb, wetting the bed, asking for a bottle, or wanting to be held.
- Have somatic symptoms of illness such as nausea, vomiting, headaches, not wanting to eat, or running a fever.
- Be quiet and withdrawn, not wanting to talk about the experience.
- Become upset easily. (Examples: Crying and whining.)
- Feel guilty that they caused the disaster because of some previous behavior.
- Feel neglected by parents who are busy trying to clean up and rebuild their lives.
- Refuse to go to school or to child care arrangements. Children may not want to be left out of their parent's sight.
- Not show any outward sign of being upset until weeks or months later.

In treating children who have experienced a storm, fire, or flood, the goals will be to help the child and the parents/caregivers. There are the immediate needs for shelter, food, and clothing. Traumatized families often need to tell and retell their account of the disaster as a means of coping with such an awful event. Children tell their story through repetitive play. The longer-term needs of the child are for security, stability, and treatment for the terror of the trauma.

I have seen children who were not victims of a tornado, but whose fears and anxieties greatly increased due to storms in their community. The emotional swath of a storm in a community is significantly larger than the immediate area hit by the disaster.

As a therapist, I consult with the parents/caregivers regarding the child's need for security and sameness, and encourage them to establish a routine as quickly as possible. Parents are usually eager for answers to "How can I help my child?" and opportunities to express their concerns about how their child is coping.

In therapy sessions, I also focus on stability and sameness. I establish a routine in therapy from the first session. Fears are the most common symptom of such children.

Play therapy sessions need to focus on understanding the child's perception of his trauma, developing effective ways of helping the child express his fears, and fostering coping skills.

Case Example Seven—Travis, Seven-Year-Old Boy, Tornado Victim

Travis was brought to me for treatment by his maternal grandmother after his home was destroyed by a tornado seven months earlier. Travis's mother was killed in the tornado and he was hospitalized overnight with cuts and a broken rib. When he came to see me, Travis was living with his grandmother.

In the initial session, Travis was active and assertive. He immediately looked for toys or items to play with. He initiated conversation and gave frequent orders such as, "Let's play this, okay?" Travis was resistant to talking about his mother, stating, "That makes me feel sick." This young boy's coping style was to take charge in an effort to control his environment. Anxiety and sadness were near the surface and he tried to avoid the pain.

Travis developed a routine in his first and second sessions. He chose the same game: *Checkers*. Travis was at the Win level; he used his own rules to make certain he beat the therapist in each game. I permitted Travis such control at the beginning of treatment as a means of coping with his anxiety. I established minimal but clear limits.

Travis chose sand tray play in the second session. He was the builder and I was the helper. Travis spent twenty minutes building a tunnel and then a bridge over it. He worked diligently to make the bridge "strong." Travis accepted my suggestions and help in strengthening the bridge. Travis' fears surfaced when the bridge showed signs of crumbling. His statement was "If the bridge falls, run to Heaven if you can." Travis ended the session with both tunnel and bridge destroyed.

In subsequent play therapy sessions, Travis continued to use symbolic play to express his trauma and grief. He then began talking about his mother, the tornado, and what the experience was like for him. Travis could only tolerate a few minutes per session to verbalize his grief.

I had him draw a picture of the tornado. Travis graphically illustrated what happened to him and his mother when their house was blown away. He drew a large,dark funnel cloud with two tiny figures. "This one up high is my mother being blown away. This one down here is me. This is the house. I drew it so you could tell it was a house, but really it was just a bunch of boards."

The latter part of treatment focused mainly on Travis's sadness at the loss of hismother, his anxiety, especially related to storms and preparation for coping with frightening events, including school fire alarm drills and community storm warning sirens. Consultation with his grandmother was an integral part of Travis's treatment. I recommended to the grandmother that Travis receive therapy for a year with sessions moving to bi-weekly and monthly as he made progress. After two months, therapy was stopped at his guardian's choice since Travis's fears and anxiety at home had lessened. School was not reporting any serious behavior problems.

CHRONIC ILLNESS (ASTHMA, SEIZURE DISORDER, FIBROMYALGIA)

The stressors of a child with a chronic illness can be overwhelming to the entire family. I am often amazed at the strength and coping ability of these children. Their parents are subject to frequent worry about their child's health, the struggle between being overprotective of the child versus allowing the child to participate in normal activities, the ambivalence of caring dearly for their child, and the fatigue of constant concern over the child's health.

Asthma

Parent and child anxiety are common characteristics when a child has moderate to severe asthma that results in life-threatening episodes, and requires frequent medication. The child tends to be overly dependent on a parent or noncompliant with his medical regimen by "forgetting" to take his medication and/or resisting physician and parent instructions. In order to be more independent, some children with asthma ignore their illness and act as if it doesn't exist. Thus, dependence/independence conflicts are a frequent developmental problem for them.

Asthma

Case Example—Anna, Ten-Year-Old Girl,

Anna was an attractive, shy girl who clung to her mother during the initial interview. She was referred by her pediatrician who specialized in allergy and asthma treatment. Anna had separation anxiety symptoms on school mornings and serious worries about forgetting a school assignment, making a mistake, or displeasing her teacher. She had almost daily complaints of stomachache and feeling sick. Her asthma was serious enough that required she take medication daily. She needed an inhaler in order to engage in any physical activity or compete in her favorite sport of soccer. My diagnostic impression was Generalized Anxiety; Anxiety Disorder due to Asthma.

Anna's treatment included cognitive behavioral therapy, play therapy, and parent consultation. She received relaxation training using thermal biofeedback. When Anna learned muscle relaxation, I introduced the desensitization method of:

- Using a thermal biofeedback trainer to teach relaxation, for Anna to reach finger temperature goal of 93 degrees or higher.
- Introducing the image of an anxiety situation from her hierarchy of school-related anxiety situations.
- Switching her thoughts from worried thought to relaxed time.
- Repeating the desensitization procedures.

- Role playing coping with worries and anxiety at school.
- Homework assignments with a relaxation tape to practice each night, and diaphragmatic breathing to practice during the school day, and at soccer practice.

Anna, who was often shy with a serious demeanor, was then able to laugh and relax during treatment.

After four sessions, Anna's mother reported a decline in the use of the inhaler for physical activity as well as in somatic complaints.

Play therapy was an integral part of Anna's treatment for anxiety. Clay modeling and drawings were her favorite activities. She identified her anxiety as "Butterflies in my stomach." Anna drew a picture of a large butterfly with signs that said, "You forgot," "You didn't remember," "Don't make a mistake," "Don't forget your work," and "Oh, no, it's a school day."

I guided Anna to identify pleasant feelings of "Happy butterflies" and "Scary butterflies." With clay, she made bright-colored butterflies for "happy" ones and dark-colored ones for "scary" butterflies. She worked at identifying small butterflies in her stomach as signals to help her remember important tasks. At that time, Anna said her worries, on a one to five scale, had decreased from threes and fours to twos. Her coping skills increased significantly by the end of the twelfth session.

Anna's mother reported few somatic complaints

of stomach pain and "feeling sick" on school mornings. Anna was more able to recognize her worries early, face her fears. She was able to change worrying thoughts such as "I'm afraid I will forget an assignment and my teacher will be mad at me" to "I do my assignments as good as I can. If I forget an assignment, I talk to my teacher to see what I can do. Now I think about something fun to do."

Regular treatment was terminated with booster sessions available on an as-needed basis. Separation-from-mother anxiety was still present but Anna was doing quite well in school adjustment. Anna's use of an inhaler for asthma decreased by 50%.

Seizure Disorder

Case Example Nine—Samuel, Ten-Year-Old Boy

Medical diagnosis of complex seizure disorder partially controlled by medication, and mild mental handicap. He wore a helmet to protect him from head injury when he had a seizure.

Samuel and his father were referred to me for behavioral treatment for problems of noncompliance with his medicine regimen, and power struggles with his father and caregivers regarding eating, and daily rules.

Samuel had developed skills in passive-aggressive behavior and persistence in resisting authority. There were periodic serious behavior problems in his special education class. Samuel also had depression symptoms related to infrequent contact with his mother. Parent consultation with his father was a necessary component of Samuel's treatment.

Samuel loved to play with the puppets. He used puppet play to interact with me and to express his moods of laughter, sadness and anger. Samuel, as most mentally handicapped children do, wanted sameness. He looked for his favorite puppets each session and repeated his play themes often. He used the mother and baby sheep to act out his sadness regarding his absentee mother. He liked to use the lion puppet to express his fear and anger. He used the bird puppet to express helplessness and sometimes to express his desire for freedom and independence.

A play doctor's kit was used to help the "sick" puppet. Samuel usually wanted me to take the doctor's role, but sometimes he was the doctor. Providing support and nurture for Samuel and regular consultation with his father regardng his medical status, and management of behavioral and emotional problems were a part of his treatment. Samuel's seizure disorder was never well-controlled by medication. Samuel did respond well to play therapy which provided him a time of acceptance, opportunity for emotional release, and attachment to the therapist.

Samuel is an example of a multiple-handicapped child who needed ongoing care. He had periods of mild improvement in compliance at home and school, and decreased depression. But family stress was high and Samuel's behavior and emotional problems, along with his seizure disorder, made long-term progress difficult.

Case Example Three—Jimmy, Seven-Year-Old Boy, Seizure Disorder and Behavior Problems

Jimmy was referred by his pediatric neurologist. He presented with serious behavior problems at school, including verbal and physical aggression toward peers.

Medical problems, such as a seizure disorder, tend to greatly affect a child's self-esteem. Having "Something wrong with my body" can lead a child to think he is damaged goods. Body image significantly affects the way a child views him- or herself.

From the diagnostic interview, I had the impression that some of Jimmy's anger and behavior problems were a reaction to having several seizures in the past six months. His drawings, responses on the Sentence Completion Test and his free play themes confirmed this impression.

Information and education regarding Jimmy's seizure disorder were an early part of his treatment. I took time with Jimmy to discover how much he knew about his illness, and his medications, and to answer his questions.

Jimmy's treatment then moved to management of his anger and his peer conflicts. Play therapy provided him an outlet to express his fears and anger in an acceptable manner. I also used free play time as a reinforcer for Jimmy's weekly progress in controlling his aggressive behavior.

Jimmy is an example of how educating child and parents about the child's medical condition can decrease fear and anger, increase compliance with a medical regimen and increase responsiveness to therapy.

Chronic Pain

Case Example Four—Pamela, Eight-Year-Old Girl, Chronic Headaches, Fibromyalgia

Pamela's pediatrician referred her to me for treatment on managing her chronic pain. Her medical history was significant. She had had headaches since her pre-school years and night terrors since she was four. Her chronic pain included headaches, neck and back pain. Her medical diagnosis included fibromyalgia and attention deficit disorder. Pamela was an attractive girl with superior intelligence. She had learned to live with pain and tended to ignore her headaches except at night time.

Her treatment consisted of behavioral medicine techniques, play therapy, and parent consultation. Relaxation training with thermal biofeedback was the main focus. Play therapy was also helpful.

In each session, Pamela was eager to switch from a focus on her medical problems to play. Joint activities were her favorites, including table games. Pamela used sand tray play in one session to express her aggressive impulses. She chose a war theme, then built a mountain that she knocked down. She concluded with a peaceful farm land. Pamela's mother reported that she frequently became angry at her five-year-old sister and would hit her. Her parents provided Pamela an outlet for her frustrations by enrolling her in Taekwondo classes.

After two months of therapy, Pamela's headache pain decreased to a "one or two" level on a five-point scale. She was sleeping better at night and had "Three good friends" instead of only one when treatment began. Her more positive outlook was evident in a storytelling session in the last month of her three-month treatment.

Pamela used clay to make a caterpillar struggling out of a cocoon. Her story of metamorphosis described how the caterpillar worked and pushed its way out of the cocoon and "Was able to fly and eat nectar." I interpreted her story to be Pamela's wish for nurturing and freedom from pain. The story was also an expression of Pamela's outlook that she was improving and gaining in freedom and independence.

LIFE THREATENING ILLNESS (CYSTIC FIBROSIS, HEART DISEASE, CANCER)

Cystic Fibrosis

Case Example One—Ron, Fourteen-Year-Old Boy

Ron's was one of the more difficult cases I have treated. He was living in long-term foster care. Abandoned by his biological parents as a young child (at least partially because of his cystic fibrosis), Ron was an angry child who avoided attachments. He was described by his foster mother as having an "I don't care" attitude.

Ron underachieved at school, had frequent behavior problems there and at home, and tended to alienate his peers through his verbal and physical aggression. He had no close friends. The only attachment Ron had was to his foster mother who was strict but caring.

In therapy Ron demanded attention. He was used to getting a negative reaction to his rude and demanding statements. He told me, "Go buy me some candy . . . I don't like your office . . . don't you have any new games?"

Initially Ron was not interested in talking about his emotions, his health, or his behavior. He denied having any behavior problems at school, said he hated school, denied that he had been verbally aggressive with children in his foster homes. Ron was more comfortable with play therapy techniques of drawings and games. I used therapeutic games to teach social skills including taking turns, playing fair, receiving quick feedback when his conversation was appropriate (i.e., "Ron, I liked it when you said, 'Good move' about that *Checkers* move") and when it was rude (i.e., "Ron, I didn't like it when you hollered, 'This is a stupid old game!'")

In time Ron moved from only shallow conversation to more honest statements. He revealed his fears, anger, and loneliness. He said, "My (biological) parents didn't want me because I was sick a lot." Ron knew enough about his illness to realize he probably would die young. "Why should I study in school? I probably won't live long." While I was seeing him, Ron witnessed the death of an eighteen-year-old foster sibling from cystic fibrosis. Ron was not interested in making any future plans. He lived only for the now because, in his mind, there was little future for him.

Ron's play therapy provided an outlet for him to express his fears and anger to an adult in a setting that was less destructive and alienating than his behavior at home and school. Play therapy addressed his oppositional behavior with the goal of increasing his awareness of his emotions, and more appropriate expression. Ron had to move from his foster home because of aggressive behavior toward other children. Progress was minimal in the four months I saw him.

Case Example Two—Grant, Fourteen-Year-Old Boy

Grant was referred to me for school underachievement, depression, anger outbursts, periodic verbal aggression toward a teacher, and strong sibling aggression toward his eleven-year-old brother. Both Grant and his brother were adopted.

Grant was diagnosed as ADHD and was on psychostimulant medication that improved his concentration and impulsiveness. He was diagnosed with a mild degree of cystic fibrosis at the time I began treatment with him. He was very small for his age and sensitive about his size.

Treatment included behavior management, play therapy, and parent consultation. Grant was emotionally immature; he was eager for play therapy games, clay and animals and sand tray play. Regression to elementary-school level was evident in his play. Play therapy sessions focused on his self-concept of being different, of having something wrong with him, of his nurturing needs, and of his difficulty with social skills.

Grant was eager to have my attention and involvement in his play activities. He accepted my suggestions regarding peer relations and was responsive to the behavior management program I instituted. I included consultation with Grant and his parents about his cystic fibrosis and treatment. Grant accepted his diagnosis and was generally compliant with his medication.

In the summer, puberty began. Grant grew several inches taller that summer and fall. His behavior improved as he no longer considered himself "a runt," and as he developed a circle of friends. Regression declined. His therapy themes became more age appropriate.

Grant was seen for four sessions during the fall semester. By the last session, his grades and behavior had significantly improved. This was a case where treatment was greatly enhanced by puberty.

Heart Disease

Treatment for children with heart disease involves the entire family. Fear and anxiety are likely the primary emotions: Parents are worried and frightened for their child. The child responds to the parents' fears, and tries to cope with extended medical treatment and fear of the unknown. Siblings wonder "Is my brother/sister very sick? Will the same thing happen to me?" Or, they feel ignored by parents whose focus is on the sick child. Play therapy can provide an outlet for sick children.

Drawings with storytelling, puppet play, bibliotherapy—all these can be useful. The child is provided an opportunity to express fear, anger, and sadness but also hope, love, and care. Books about children coping with illnesses can be useful. Children need information about their disease, opportunities to ask questions, and to talk. Children can handle the truth about their illness better than a secret that is not discussed with the child.

The main fear of children with life-threatening illness is that of being alone. They need to know that their family is there for them: To laugh, to cry, to comfort, to stay with them.

Cancer/Tumors

Case Example Two—Marie, Five-Year-Old Girl, Who Had Brain Surgery

I will never forget little Marie, who was referred to me by her pediatrician and parents. Marie had undergone two brain surgeries in three months. She had some paralysis on the left side of her face (Bell's Palsy) as a result of the surgeries. The referral was to assist Marie in coping with recovery from brain surgery, her concerns about her facial appearance, some regression, and fears resulting from her painful medical procedures.

I admired Marie for her adaptability in adjusting to her medical problems, in her assertiveness and eagerness for life. On her initial appointment, Marie was apprehensive about what this doctor would be like. When she saw my office and the toys, she quickly adapted to seeing her "Feelings doctor."

Marie was friendly and eager to initiate themes

in play therapy. She drew a picture of her family and wanted to show me she could write numbers and her name. She used the dollhouse and clay to make animals. Prior to therapy, Marie made some disturbing statements about her physical appearance since her surgery, including, "I have a stupid smile" (from her left side facial paralysis), "I'm ugly," "I'm retarded," "My brain is dead," but she demonstrated remarkable honesty and coping skills. Her mother reported that when Marie noticed a person staring at her in a store, she looked at the person and said, "I had brain surgery."

In therapy sessions, Marie demonstrated little self consciousness about her appearance. She spent most of her time in creative play and in "Getting on with life" post surgery. She wanted most of the session time for herself and for her mother to wait in the reception room. She liked to share what she had done in her session with her mother later.

In the third session, Marie separated easily from her mother and expressed her autonomy needs. She chose "Wild animals" and tamed them by putting clay saddles on them. I introduced a storm scene; Marie's response was that the animals died. But then the animals were alive again and she continued her theme of taming them. Marie minimized her hospital fears by stating, "The only thing I was afraid of in the hospital was a bug." She noted her mother's and father's fears by stating, "My Mom and Dad were really scared when I fell down in the store after my operation."

I focused on her fears about the surgery and medical procedures. She responded well. Marie's outlook was to talk about them briefly, then move on to the present and the future.She seemed to sense how precious her time was and wanted to enjoy life as much as possible. She had strong family support and made remarkable adjustment during the six sessions in which I saw her.

Marie made a good recovery from her surgeries and did well in preschool and kindergarten. Two years later, I saw her mother. She sadly reported that Marie died suddenly from a brain stem anomaly unrelated to her brain tumor surgeries. Marie was seven years old. I will never forget this remarkable, brave little girl.

PRACTICAL EXERCISE

Develop a treatment plan for a child who has experienced each of these environmental stressors.

1. Violence (crime, abuse)
   Description of the Child:

   Specific Problems:

   Treatment Plans:

   Progress and Comments:

2. Natural Disasters (storms, flood, fire)
   Description of the Child:

   Specific Problems:

   Treatment Plans:

   Progress and Comments:

3. Chronic Illness
   Description of the Child:

   Specific Problems:

   Treatment Plans:

   Progress and Comments:

4. Life-Threatening Illness
   Description of the Child:

   Specific Problems:

   Treatment Plans:

   Progress and Comments:

CHILDQUOTE

Complimenting Mom

Five-year-old Rachel's mother did not enjoy cooking. It was not her strength; she was employed outside the home and was glad for the father to prepare most meals while she did other household chores. One morning, Rachel's father was complaining about how poor a cook her mother was. Rachel quickly defended her mother. She held up a Corn Flakes cereal box and stated, "But, Mom, you're good at cooking cereal."

Part IV

Behavior Therapy

11

MANAGING DIFFICULT BEHAVIOR IN THE OFFICE, SCHOOL AND COMMUNITY

Description and Intervention

Child therapists are faced with managing behavior problems on a daily basis. Let's look at some case examples and see if they seem similar to your cases. In this chapter, I will share the approach I take in treating difficult behavior. The five case examples describe how I apply behavior management to various types of behavior problems.

Case Example One—Dustin, Five-Year-Old Boy

Dustin was referred for severe social behavior prob-

lems in kindergarten and day care as well as for oppositional defiant behavior at home and school. He
entered my office reluctantly and hid behind his
mother as she led him into the room. Dustin fell to
the floor, and hit and kicked at his mom as she guided
him to the sofa. His mother was embarrassed, frustrated, and angry at her resistive child. Dustin refused
to talk to me and screeched loudly with unintelli-
gible sounds, although his speech was clear when he
chose to speak.

His mother and preschool teacher reported severe behavior problems at school. Dustin chose to
play by himself, hit other children who came into
his play area, and he refused to sit or participate in
small group activities. He had run out of the classroom on several occasions.

Diagnosed with ADHD, Dustin frequently refused to take his psychostimulant medication. When
he was compliant and in an established routine, he
demonstrated good concentration, strength in visual
motor areas of block building, and near average speech
and language ability.

Case Example Two—Benjamin, Six-Year-Old Boy

On the first visit, Benjamin quickly displayed his aggressiveness. When I greeted him and his mother in
the reception room, Benjamin looked me sternly in
the eye, refused my offered handshake, and shouted,
"No! Leave me alone."

Upon entering my office with his mother for the

family interview, Benjamin went straight to the toy cabinet, opened the doors, and began exploring. He ignored his mother's commands to sit with her. When Benjamin did talk to me, he spoke loudly and with a gruff, angry voice as he held a plastic space tube, "What's this dumb thing?"

Benjamin's mother was anxious and repeatedly instructed him to "Stop that. Put that down. Answer the doctor." Benjamin ignored her commands and continued his intrusive behavior.

Benjamin's kindergarten classroom achievement was at average to above average level. But, he had been suspended for three days for his daily aggressive behavior of hitting other students.

Later in that first visit, Benjamin's mood changed to cooperative. He concentrated on his assignment of a Kinetic Family Drawing, was concerned that his drawing be just right, and spoke in a normal tone with a polite manner.

Case Example Three—Faith, Five-Year-Old Girl

Faith was presented with separation anxiety. Her father and mother were concerned that Faith had become anxious and fearful when she was apart from her mother. She was a strong-willed child who was persistent about her likes and dislikes. She was resistive to preschool and mother's day out saying, "I don't want to go. I want to stay with you, Mommy."

On the first visit to my office, Faith wanted her mother to stay with her. Her mother was anxious;

she tried to keep her daughter calm and sat close to her. Mother did not want to leave the room, fearful that Faith would become upset if she left.

Case Example Four—Arnold, Eleven-Year-Old Boy

Arnold was referred to me for therapy due to a need for anger management and because of lying behavior. He had been to In-School Suspension (ISS) for verbal aggression behavior of interrupting and talking back to his teacher, disrupting the classroom, and arguing with other students. Arnold's grades dropped from As and Bs in the fifth grade to Bs and Cs in the sixth grade. His parents were also concerned with Arnold's increased lying. He denied doing anything wrong in class and told his mother that he had no homework assignments. Arnold also expressed verbal aggression toward his parents on several occasions, including telling them, "I hate you."

In his first therapy session, Arnold was socially skilled, polite and easy to engage in conversation. He spoke of his willingness to "work" on his anger. But any improvement was short lived, for his impulsive, angry behavior continued at school.

Arnold displayed the same social skills in my office that his parents and teachers reported. He had a winsome personality. His teacher liked him despite his oppositional and argumentative classroom behavior. Arnold's mother described him as having sudden mood changes: From being a "a sweet, lovable child with a sudden change to being hostile, angry and oppositional." She expressed fear that Arnold's verbal aggression could escalate to physical aggression.

Case Example Five—Maddie, Three-Year-Old Girl

Maddie was diagnosed with autism. She had no intelligible language and expressed her desires and emotions at the level of a one-year-old, but her gross motor skills were above average.

In my office on the first and second appointments, Maddie was restless, continually roaming around the room. She found the sand tray box, stood on it and began to jump up and down. She climbed on top of the testing table and jumped off it. Her parents spent much time trying to keep her under control. Maddie screamed in anger and hit at her mother when she was stopped from disruptive behavior.

How do you manage the difficult behaviors of children like Dustin, Benjamin, Faith, Arnold, and Maddie?

First, limits must be established. I have never seen an out-of-control child who was happy. It is frightening not to be able to control your own behavior, whether you're a child or an adult.

Behavior therapy principles are the recommended treatment in setting boundaries and limits for children. Play therapy has a role in working with such children, but behavior therapy is primary. Use behavior therapy based on these established learning theory principles:

GUIDELINES FOR BEHAVIOR MANAGEMENT

When you wish to change a child's behavior, you have four choices:

1. **Reward behavior** when you like what that person is doing. Use positive reinforcement.
2. **Ignore behavior** when you don't like what that person is doing.
3. **Punish behavior** that you can't ignore. Use aversive consequences.
4. **Teach new behavior** when you want the person to learn new responses. Use modeling and imitation learning.

Principles of Behavior Management

The focus is on behavior—*learned* behavior.

1. To *increase* a particular behavior, use *positive reinforcement* (reward).

   Positive reinforcer: Anything that increases the likelihood that a behavior will be repeated.

   Primary (unlearned) reinforcers: Food, water, air.

   (Example: A favorite snack for satisfactory behavior.)

   Secondary (learned) reinforcers: Attention, praise, privilege, success, money.

   Attention from an adult is a powerful reinforcer for most children.

(Example: Praise for completing a chore.)

2. Rewarding improvements leads to further improvements (shaping).

(Example: A child praised for helping an adult put her toys away, then praised for putting toys away on her own.)

3. Reward immediately (as quickly as possible). Small immediate rewards are more powerful than large, delayed rewards.

4. Begin with frequent rewards to establish behavior, then move to occasional rewards to maintain behavior.

(Example: A child receives praise and a token for not hitting for one hour. With improvement, move the child to every two hours, then four hours, and then reward for maintaining the behavior for an entire day.)

5. Reward consistently. Work for 95% to 100% consistency by caregivers.

Without consistency, behavior is not likely to improve.

6. To teach new behavior, use *modeling** (imitation learning) as in "Monkey see, monkey do," and practice (behavioral rehearsal).

Modeling (imitation learning) is a source of positive and negative learning.
Positive example: When an adult expresses frustration clearly by telling the child: "I'm angry at you because you hit Jimmy."
(Negative example: Yelling when mad.)

Behavior rehearsal: Have child practice the behavior you have demonstrated.

(Example: Showing a child how to catch a ball and practicing with the child.)

7. To reduce a behavior, use ignoring (non-reward). Example: Not giving attention when the child interrupts but using a hand gesture without eye contact to show "stop." Thank the child for waiting and then give attention.

8. To reduce a behavior, use an effective punishment (when behavior cannot be ignored). Punishment should be administered consistently without strong anger and with the least possible amount of talking.

   Time out (loss of freedom). The rule of thumb is a one-minute timeout for each year of age.

   (Example: A six-year-old child is given a six-minute time out for throwing a toy across the room.)

   Overcorrection (repeating a corrective activity).

   (Examples: The child is required to wash and re-wash the floor three times after he tracks mud into the house, or have the child who runs down the hall practice walking down the hall slowly three times. This is behavior rehearsal of the desired behavior.)

APPLYING BEHAVIOR THERAPY

Need for Assessment

See Chapter 2 for guidance in conducting a thorough assessment.

Obtaining an accurate diagnosis is necessary for an effective treatment plan.

Behavior therapy usually works best within a multimodal treatment context.

If a child has ADHD, then effective medication plus behavior therapy is likely the treatment of choice.

If a child is depressed or anxious, play therapy, along with cognitive-behavior or behavior therapy, is the likely choice.

If a child is grieving over significant losses, grief therapy should be included.

If a child has a learning disability or developmental delay, special education services and consultation with teachers and parents is an important component of treatment.

Applying behavior therapy may be the immediate need, but accurate assessing will help you determine what additional therapies are warranted: medication, play therapy, family therapy, cognitive behavior therapy, grief therapy, parent consultation, and school consultation.

Reinforcement History

What activities, objects, or attention does the child really like? Which does the child dislike or avoid?

The child's perception determines whether something is reinforcing or is punishing. There are general reinforcers that most children respond to, such as attention and praise, but it is important to know what this particular child finds rewarding or aversive.

I recommend a reinforcement menu gathered from the child, the parent(s), and your observations. The menu is used to provide various, multiple reinforcers that are effective because the child is likely to tire of only one reinforcer.

Limit Setting/Rules

Rules need to be stated clearly. I recommend having few rules, but enough to maintain clear limits. Children will remember four to six main rules, but will have difficulty with twenty. I like to ask children to tell me what the rules are at their house. I then ask the parents the same question and look for agreement and disagreement between parent and child. Rules should have as many *Dos* as *Don'ts*.

I often tell my young patients, "I have two rules in my office. One, no hitting, kicking or spitting and I won't hit, kick or spit on you. Two, when you are finished with a toy, put it back before you get another one." I want the child to know right away what the boundaries are and what is acceptable and unacceptable behavior.

Parents come to therapists feeling a loss of control over their children. I want to assist parents in establishing limits and gaining a sense of control over their child's behavior. Then, parent and child have time to enjoy each other, to hug, to play, to laugh.

Consistency: A Necessity

Applying behavior management techniques with consistency leads to success. Inconsistency leads to failure. I want children to know what they can expect from me as their therapist, and what to expect from their parents and caregivers. When parents disagree regarding rules, I work with them to come to a compromise so that one parent doesn't undermine the other parent's authority.

In divorced families, it is hard to have consistency in two different homes. It is harder for a child to adjust to two sets of rules. Consistency in this case means, "At Mom's house, these are the rules; at Dad's house, these are the rules." The child can learn to comply with these rules, particularly if parents don't undermine each other's authority.

Record keeping/Compliance

Keep records of progress or lack of progress in changing target behaviors. A friend passed this wisdom on to me years ago: "It's not just what you expect; it's what you inspect." This applies to behavior therapy. I ask parents to record progress or the lack thereof. I check with the child and with the parent(s) each session. How compliant parent(s) are in applying the techniques is a big determiner of success or failure in establishing behavior control, and is diagnostic in family dynamics.

As therapists, we need to encourage and support parents in their working the treatment plan: Reinforce parents for reinforcing children. That's the way to work. Praise and encouragement are usually effective reinforcers (rewards) for parents.

Adapting Therapy

Your behavior treatment plan is likely to need fine tuning. Just as a television screen needs adjusting to get the best picture, so do behavior plans. The feedback I get from parents and caregivers helps me make alterations so that the therapy for this child and this parent can be most effective. Be a good behavioral scientist and use the feedback from the child and parent(s) to adjust your treatment.

Self Control is the Goal

The main goal of behavior therapy is to help increase a child's self control. Some parents object to "Rewarding kids for being good." They may say, "I want my kid to do what's right just because it's right, not for the reward he gets."

I agree that the ultimate goal is for moral behavior based on the principle of "Do unto others as you would have others do unto you." But, behavior therapy is a deliberate, planned application of rewards and punishment to help children who do not have good self control make progress in controlling their behavior. Children can grow up to learn to reward themselves for moral behavior. However, most of us adults still need praise, encouragement and some material rewards to help us maintain appropriate self control. For sure, most children need such reinforcers.

The goal is to establish the limits necessary to help children gain more self control so they can experience success at home, at school and in their community.

CASE EXAMPLES

Case Example One—Dustin, Five-Year-Old Boy (See page 249)

Dustin was diagnosed with ADHD, selective mutism, physical aggression, and social immaturity. He was a very difficult case. Establishing some control of his behavior in my office was immediate. Referral to a physician for medication management was the next step. Consultation with his mother and school regarding his aggressive behavior and poor social skills were major components of his treatment.

In therapy, I used differential reinforcement to decrease Dustin's withdrawal and oppositional behavior. I ignored and didn't respond to Dustin when he hid behind an office chair and refused to talk to his mother or me. This off-task behavior was typical at the beginning of the behavior therapy session. I reinforced with attention, showed interest in his play activities, and talked to Dustin when he engaged in on-task behavior of cooperative block building play and use of his normal conversational voice.

I used a firm voice to correct Dustin when he hit at his mother. I reviewed the school teachers' weekly report of positive and negative behavior. During the school year, Dustin made moderate progress: From isolating himself from all the other children and becoming physically aggressive toward a child who attempted to play with him, he moved to periods of sitting at the same work station with other children and occasionally working with them.

Parent consultation with his stressed single mother, Ms. Grimes, who had little social support was an important cause of improvement. I wanted Ms. Grimes to have some control of her own behavior. Dustin's defiance was totally frustrating her. She tended to reject his clinging behavior, spent much time trying to get him to mind her. Little affection was evident between mother and son. She was also over-stressed with frequent phone calls from school and day care regarding Dustin's aggressive and out-of-control behavior. Parent consultation and family therapy included:

1. Modeling the differential reinforcement of ignoring off-task behavior and attending to on-task behavior;
2. Providing emotional support and guidance in parenting skills;
3. Teaching anger management skills;
4. Encouraging consistency in applying rules with Dustin, and
5. Joint play therapy activities with mother and son in the office. Dustin responded to positive play activity with his mother. She was able to relax and give Dustin some approval and positive attention.

Dustin's behavior, social and emotional problems required special education placement. I provided guidance to the mother and teacher regarding Dustin's developmental levels and temperament. Socially and emotionally Dustin was functioning at the three-year-old level. He preferred solitary play. He did not know how to interact with other children except "Leave me alone or I'll hit you." Dustin's teacher adjusted his schedule so that he was not required to join large group time. Dustin had only his desk area to work at.

When he showed interest in a group activity, Dustin was accepted but not singled out. He reduced the amount of refusals to cooperate with his teachers' instructions. By shaping methods, Dustin learned to notice the group activity, to sit next to the group, and to participate in some small group time. Progress was slow, but Dustin was able to remain in school.

Continued consultation with a child psychiatrist for medication management was part of Dustin's treatment.

In treating a child like Dustin, I use behavior therapy, family and/or parent consultation, play therapy, referral for medication management (if indicated from assessment), and school consultation. Treatment goals need to be realistic. The therapist must be persistent and consistent in the application of behavior therapy.

Case Example Two—Benjamin, Six-Year-Old Boy (See page 250)

Benjamin was diagnosed with severe oppositional behavior and divorce adjustment problems.

How did I manage Benjamin's difficult behavior? In the initial interview, I used ignoring, differential reinforcement, and establishing basic rules for the office. It was clear that Benjamin's initial response to social situations was a fight response, and that the usual mother-son interaction was that mother repeated verbal commands in an anxious voice while Benjamin ignored or argued with her.

Benjamin was a middle child; he lived with his single mother and two brothers, aged eight and five. His parents separated two years previously, when Benjamin was four, and the divorce had only been final for four months. Benjamin had weekly contact with his father. Benjamin's parenting was inconsistent since he sometimes received close supervision, but often was ignored by his busy parents until he acted out.

Benjamin was a first grader in a private school with a committed, caring teacher. His physical aggression toward peers was a daily serious problem. At home, he was often physically aggressive toward his brothers, picked on by his older brother, and was frequently noncompliant and argued with his mother.

When he was verbally aggressive toward me in the reception room, I ignored Benjamin and talked to his mother as we walked down the hall to my office. Benjamin followed with little protest. Sometimes he grabbed toys in the office and ignored his mother's repeated "Don't do that" commands. I took the toy from him and established limits stating, "Benjamin, we are going to visit for ten minutes (as I set the egg timer), then you may choose one toy or game. The rule is, 'When you finish with one toy, put it away before you get another one.'" Benjamin tested me several times. I used non-verbal responses primarily, and short, direct instructions without repeating them. My actions modeled a different approach to her son for the mother, and established a consistent behavior management program.

Differential reinforcement used was non-reinforcement (ignoring) of the attention-getting off-task behavior. I used limited eye contact and mostly non-verbal responses. But, I made immediate eye contact and gave positive attention for on-task behaviors such as making appropriate statements, asking questions, using a less hostile voice and complying with my or his mother's requests.

In one-on-one time, I found Benjamin wanting to do well in his Kinetic Family Drawing, demonstrating good concentration and speaking in a pleasant voice. Positive reinforcement of attention and approval was used during this time.

I worked with Benjamin's mother to develop a token system for school first, and later included home behaviors: Daily Behavior Report Card was implemented: His teacher completed the card every day and Benjamin brought the card home. See Appendix 6 for Daily Behavior Report Card forms for home and for school.

Benjamin received two minutes of "Benjamin Time" at home for every excellent or good rating. There were seven time periods times three behaviors for a possible score of 21 per day.

A menu of desired behaviors was developed with Benjamin's input and his mother's approval. Privileges included in the menu were: play time with mother, time with a computer game, having a friend over, television time.

Benjamin's mother cooperated in record keeping with my encouragement and a review every session. Use of the point system was a good behavior management program for a child like Benjamin.

He made mild improvement at school within two weeks, earning some privilege time each day, but his daily physical aggression continued, most often during recess. My focus was on helping his mother be consistent in monitoring the behavior program and giving daily "Benjamin Time" to her son. Benjamin's father attended two sessions, but was not consistently involved in the treatment plan.

Benjamin's mother was responsive to my directives to talk less, give no more than two reminders and to be consistent in following through with the rules. I instructed her to work toward a consistent, daily routine so that Benjamin could predict what was going to happen, and to reduce their hectic schedule. Benjamin had compulsive traits. He resisted any sudden change. He wanted to know his schedule. I also told her to give Benjamin limited choices of behavior for his oppositional traits.

It takes consistent application of a behavior management program with a child like Benjamin to reduce such serious behavior problems. After the behavior plan was implemented, I was able to use play therapy with Benjamin. We focused on his emotional problems of fear and anger related to his parents' divorce to reduce some of his hostility.

Case Example Three—Faith, Five-Year-Old Girl (See page 251)

Faith was diagnosed with separation anxiety. Desensitization of separation fears is the usual behavior treatment for separation anxiety. I want to be sure that the child has not and is not having extended periods of time away from the parents without a known caregiver. When extended, stressful separations occur, the preferred treatment is to reduce such situational stress rather than desensitization.

I prefer to be a source of positive reinforcement for an anxious child. However, as in Faith's case, sometimes I assume the aversive role. The goal is that the child and parent will overcome their fears. It is more important for the child to get better than for me to be liked.

Faith's separation anxiety had become severe in the past month before I saw her. Her mother had some health problems, was stressed from caring for Faith and an infant, and gave ambivalent signals to Faith of "Go to your class/I'm afraid you'll be upset if I leave." Her father was worried and frustrated with both mother and daughter. On the first session in my office, the mother expressed fear that Faith wouldn't stay apart from her for even a few minutes.

On the second visit, I addressed the separation fears with a behavioral intervention and took the aversive role. The session began with fifteen minutes of joint time with Faith and her mother to be followed by twenty minutes of play therapy with Faith alone.

When I asked the mother to leave for twenty minutes, she was hesitant. Faith responded by wanting her mother to stay. I insisted that the mother leave; I would come and get her in twenty minutes.

When the mother left my office for the reception room, I rolled my desk chair in front of the door to prevent Faith from leaving. She became angry and yelled, "I want my Mommy," repeatedly.

When I wouldn't open the door, despite her screaming, Faith hid behind the reclining chair and yelled, "You're mean!"

When this didn't work, Faith upped the ante, using kindergarten-type playground verbal assaults.

"You're mean! And you're stupid!"

After yelling this several times, Faith brought out the heavy artillery.

"You're mean! You're stupid! And you stink!"

I acknowledged her fears and anger at me but kept my word; she stayed in my office for twenty minutes. Faith cried, but was quieter the last five minutes.

When the timer rang, I told Faith, "Your twenty minutes are up; let's go get your mother." Faith's mother had a hard time with her own anxiety and was eager to see her daughter. Faith ran to her mother and announced, "He's mean."

I explained the reason for my behavior and the need for a child to face fears, beginning with a short separation, then increasing the time. I would not have used this approach if Faith had experienced a trauma such as abuse, violence, accident, storm, or death. Faith's background information, and my diagnostic interview, indicated she suffered from separation anxiety without a trauma experience. Desensitization was the treatment of choice from my experience.

The third session called for the same time schedule. Faith accepted the twenty-minute play time without her mother. She was not happy to see me, but she accepted the separation without any strong, emotional reaction. Mother was still anxious but her child had responded to limit setting, and to her mother's refusal to be manipulated.

The next step was to work with the parents and teacher to determine the length of time of separation from the parent, and to increase that time by increments of approximately 50 percent. In her parents' presence, I told Faith, "It is a hard job to face your fears. It can be very scary and takes courage. But if you stay with it, the fears will get smaller." I also coached her parents with the effort to explain how fear is lessened and how it is extinguished through learning principles. I encouraged and supported parents in implementing such treatment and sticking with it.

Play therapy is a helpful part of treating separation anxiety and is discussed in Chapter 8.

Case Example Four—Arnold, Eleven-Year-Old Boy, (See page 252)

Arnold was diagnosed with anger, verbal aggression (primarily at school), lying behavior, and decreased school achievement. How do you work with a child like Arnold with oppositional defiant behavior?

Arnold was a handsome, socially skilled child who was having behavior problems of verbal aggression toward teachers and students, missing homework assignments, and lying to his parents about his school work. Despite serious anger problems at school, Arnold's teachers all liked him; he had the ability to manipulate adults. I noted this in initial therapy sessions. Arnold knew how to say the things he thought adults wanted to hear.

My treatment plan included setting three-month goals with Arnold and his mother, and development of a behavior program in which Arnold earned privileges based on his weekly school reports about his behavior and his academic performance. Arnold's behavior was monitored through weekly consultation with his mother and Arnold in which his performance was reviewed. The primary contributor to Arnold's progress was the consistent behavior plan monitored by his mother and myself. The mother spent less time in arguing with and being manipulated by her son. Mother learned that the goal in managing Arnold was not "to make him mind" but to hold Arnold responsible for his specific behavior. The behavior plan helped her do this with less arguing and cajoling.

I used cognitive-behavioral therapy with Arnold and trained him in awareness of his anger levels, situations, and actions that increased and decreased his anger, role playing of options in expressing his anger, and relaxation exercises. I consulted with Arnold's mother on ways to reduce verbal confrontations at home, make rules and consequences clear, and to state them in writing. I talked with her about consistent implementation of rules, and suggested a daily conversation time with Arnold with a focus on relating to him rather than focusing on rules and misconduct. Arnold enjoyed such conversation time. He loved to talk. At these times it was not arguing, it was sharing conversation with his mother.

Progress tends to be slow in cases like Arnold's. The anger and verbal aggression problems had been present for more than a year when we began therapy. Persistence and consistency in parent's and therapist's implementation of behavior therapy are major.

I think it helped the mother for me to explain oppositional defiant children as having a high need to control as exhibited by Arnold's arguing and resistance to school and home rules. These children tend to clash with parents and teachers over rules and commands. Managing such a child meant avoiding head-on clashes except when absolutely necessary.

I recommended limited choices. For example, "Arnold, it's time to do your homework. Which subject do you want to do first?" "Arnold, you're talking very loud and you sound angry. Can you lower your voice and talk now, or do you need some time alone to cool down?"

Since the control need is extremely high with oppositional children like Arnold, I use control words often. Examples: "Arnold, what happened when you lost control and began yelling at your English teacher?" "How did you control yourself by waiting to talk until your teacher finished speaking?" "Can you tell me about a problem time this week when you had good control, and how you expressed your frustration?" "Can you tell me about a time when you lost control and yelled at your teacher or mother?"

He had little insight into what he did or did not do that made situations better or worse. But, after three visits, Arnold began to monitor his own behavior and how he expressed his anger. In use of the Thinking, Feeling, Doing game, Arnold dropped some of his defenses. He spoke of how he could be in a pleasant mood and change quickly to anger. He also stated his desire to be more popular at school and said, "I'm afraid of being a goody-goody kid." He noted that his friends didn't like such kids.

With the treatment program that included the

behavior management plan, parent support and guidance, and play therapy focus on lowering his defenses, Arnold showed significant improvement after three months of weekly treatment. He reduced his anger behavior, improved his classroom work and improved his relationship with his mother.

Case Example Five—Maddie, Three-Year-Old Girl (See page 253)

Maddie was diagnosed with autism. How do you treat a child like Maddie? First, I confirmed the autism diagnosis. Behavior therapy plus speech and language therapy were the treatments of choice. Parent consultation regarding diagnosis and treatment were provided. I referred the parents to the special education director of their local school system. I consulted with the coordinator of developmental preschool programs. Maddie's parents enrolled her in the preschool class for autistic children.

During the first year of treatment, I consulted with the parents regularly about Maddie's preschool program and her progress. I used behavior therapy sessions to establish a routine that reduced Maddie's disruptive behavior. I demonstrated for the mother how to increase Maddie's eye contact, how to teach her to imitate my nonverbal behavior, and how to stimulate language development using Ivan Lovaas's behavior therapy approach. I coached her mother to practice these behaviors in sessions, and daily at home. Maddie's mother and father were cooperative and compliant in homework assignments.

Within a month, Maddie's behavior in my office was very manageable. The routine was established. In each session, Maddie came into my office with her mother. She went to the toy chest to pick out her favorite toys, gave me the timer and candy dish to use later in the session, and tolerated brief training sessions.

In our first year, Maddie made a twelve-month increase in her adaptive behavior as measured by the Scales of Independent Behavior—Revised (SIB—R). She thoroughly enjoyed her developmental preschool which she attended daily. Maddie was cooperative and affectionate with her teachers. Her eye contact improved. Her toilet training was completed at home. Much of her progress was due to a fine special education preschool. My main contributions were parent education regarding treatment for autism, modeling of the homework assignments, and providing support and encouragement to Maddie's parents.

In her speech development, Maddie was able to pronounce common words, such as "Hello, goodbye, Mommy. . . ." She liked to imitate my animal sounds in puppet play. Maddie loved music and was able to sing preschool songs such as the "ABC Song"; "Twinkle, Twinkle Little Star", "One, Two, Buckle My Shoe", and "This Old Man". Her speech intelligibility was fair to poor but Maddie attempted more and more speech and improved every month. Maddie had a diagnosis of mild to moderate degree of autism. It was exciting for this therapist to see her progress, to have her eager face greet me at the beginning of each session, to interact with her and receive goodbye hugs.

In treating a child with pervasive developmental disabilities like Maddie's, it is of major importance to obtain special education enrollment and to provide consultation to school and parents. Behavior therapy is needed to manage behavior and to teach new behaviors.

The five case examples in this chapter emphasize the value of behavior management plans based on sound theoretical principles as a means of managing difficult behavior. Play therapy techniques based on behaviorial therapy are recommended in treating such children.

PRACTICAL EXERCISE

Select a child with difficult behavior problems. Develop a treatment plan with behavioral goals.
Goal #1:

Goal #2:

Goal #3:

What positive reinforcers and punishers do you plan to use? What new behavior do you plan to teach this child?

Progress Notes:

Record the date. Record the behavior changes, effective and ineffective behavior management.

CHILDQUOTE

On Being Good

Four-year-old Darrell was having difficulty conforming to the rules of his preschool. He had been in trouble several times in one day. In frustration he looked sternly at his preschool teacher and said, "I like myself just the way I am. I don't want to learn to be good."

I Don't Need Therapy

Seven-year-old Byron was reluctant to go back for therapy after a six-week interval. Byron had been treated six months for severe aggressive and angry behavior problems in school. Byron's behavior had improved significantly in the past but had worsened in the last two months. Byron told his mother, "I don't need to go to Dr. Price today. He fixed me the first time. Why do I need to come back?"

12

PARENT CONSULTATION FOR MANAGING BEHAVIOR PROBLEMS

Principles, Model, and Example

Children are always to be treated in the context of the family. Just as play therapy is the preferred method of treating most preschool and school-aged children, parent consultation is the preferred method of working with most parents. Therapists work within the family system, whether their expertise is in family therapy, marital counseling, individual therapy, play therapy, behavior therapy, psychodynamic therapy, or another theoretical model. The diagnostic assessment helps determine whether the parents need individual or marital counseling in addition to the child's treatment.

A major part of the child's treatment is parent

consultation. The goals of parent consultation include:

- To increase parenting skills in areas of nurturing and/or child management.
- To increase parents' knowledge of child development and what is reasonable to expect of their child(ren) at this age and level of development.
- To provide tools and guidance in behavior management.
- To obtain compliance in applying treatment outside the office.
- To reinforce parents for their work,
- To provide support and encouragement in coping with difficult family problems.

ASSUMPTIONS ABOUT CHILD MANAGEMENT

1. Children can teach parents how best to parent them.

   From infancy, children communicate how they like to be held and with what they are comfortable and uncomfortable. Children show us when they need more or less stimulation, more or less affection, more or less supervision, more or less freedom, more or less restriction.

2. The goal of child management is to help children have more positive control over their lives.

Power and control are major issues in parent-child relations. An example is the oppositional, strong-willed child who has an extra dose of need for control. I try to help parents disengage from major power struggles with children that tend to sidetrack effective parenting. Giving a child limited choices and holding the child responsible for her choice is preferred. The parents decide what they will do, based on the child's actions.

Another example is the child with an anger behavior problem. The treatment goal is to help the child control his behavior. I discuss with the child and parents what happens when the child lashes out in anger.

Acceptable expressions of anger are discussed. These can include:

a) Verbal expression: "I'm mad at you, Mommy, because you wouldn't let me go outside."
b) Cooling down, using the relaxation exercise of letting go of the mad feelings.
c) Time out to be alone for a few minutes,
d) Self talk, such as, "I'm mad and this is how I will show it."
e) Letting go of anger through physical activity.
f) Switching thoughts to something positive.

I ask the child and parents, "When were you/ when was your child angry and had good control of behavior? When did you/when did he lose control?" Parents are instructed to notice and compliment their child when he does show improvement in his behavior. Use of "You had good *control,* " or "You lost *control,*" are phrases I encourage parents to use in talking with their child about such behavior.

A third example is the amount of supervision needed in particular situations. If a child can play unsupervised for several minutes or an hour, a recommended parent response would be, "John, you handled playing outside with your friends for an hour. Good job!"

If the opposite occurs, "John, you had trouble playing outside for an hour; that was too long. I will check on you in thirty minutes to see how well you handle your free time."

Parents can observe and determine how long the child can be unsupervised during homework. "Mary, show me your assignment for today. Let's see how much you can do on your own. We can start with fifteen minutes. I'll check with you then. If you need help sooner, come ask me."

3. Child management involves the effective use of rewards and punishment. They need to be applied consistently and carefully, rather than haphazardly, inconsistently, and without planning. Rewards (positive reinforcement) should be dispensed more often than punishment. Reinforcement focuses on what you want the child to *do;* punishment focuses on what you want her *not to do.*

Positive reinforcement of parent attention and praise are powerful reinforcers for almost all children.

Another effective reinforcer is the child's desired behavior. I recommend the following technique, especially with a strong willed child:

Undesirable behavior (Example: Cleaning child's room) is rewarded with desirable behavior (Example: Playing with friend).

Jimmy (in demanding voice): "I'm going outside to play with Tommy."

Parent: "When you have cleaned your room, you can play for an hour."

Jimmy: "I'll clean my room afterward."

Parent: "You can play as soon as your room is clean."

The basic principle is: "When you ____, you can ____." For example, "When you do your work, you can play (desired activity)."

This is more effective that the "If you don't ____, you can't ____." As in "If you don't clean your room right now, you won't get to play today."

This technique can reduce some power struggles with children. The child gains freedom of choice as soon as she completes her job.

The parent does not have to search for which reward to promise. The child has already said the reward she wants. If the child's desired reward is unacceptable, the parents let the child choose from an acceptable reward list.

Example: Tony wants to go shopping for a toy as soon as he cleans his room. His father says, "Tony, I'm not willing to take you shopping this morning. We can go Saturday. When you clean your room, you have free time to do what you want for an hour."

4. Behavior therapy's goal is to begin with the external rewards necessary to manage the problem behavior, and move to internal rewards as the child progresses in self control.

Parents often want children to behave by the golden rule of "Do unto others as you would have others do unto you." But the child may be operating under another rule such as, "Do to others before they can do to you," "Might makes right," "Rules are for other kids, not for me," or "Don't get caught."

Some parents object to behavior management programs stating, "I don't want to bribe my kids," "I don't want them to think they'll only do something if they get a reward," or "You shouldn't have to pay kids to do right."

I explain to the parents that they are already rewarding and punishing their children for their behavior. I also point out that much adult behavior is influenced by external rewards and punishment, i.e., paychecks, fines, praise and encouragement from others. Child management's purpose is to use rewards and punishment more effectively.

Parents may reward a child with the most attention when he is misbehaving. Such negative attention tends to increase the likelihood the child will act out again in order to gain the parents' attention. When a parent takes time to play with a child or notice a child's accomplishment and attention requests such as "Dad, watch me . . . Mom, see what I did . . .," the parent is providing positive reinforcement that increases the chance that the child will repeat the desired behavior.

The goal is to move from fewer external rewards to more internal rewards, such as the desire to please parents and significant adults, pride in doing a task well, or the desire to treat others as you want them to treat you. Material rewards are mainly used to obtain improvement.

The guiding principle is: Use as much external reward as needed to change behavior; then move to as few external rewards as needed to maintain the desired behavior.

RESOURCES

The following are some parent training resources available to use in parent consultation:

Defiant Children—A Clinician's Manual for Assessment and Parent Training, Second Edition, by Russell A. Barkley, Ph.D., Guilford Press, New York, 1997.

Dr. Barkley sets forth the sequence of procedures for training parents in child management skills. The book contains ten guidelines for therapists in conducting each step of the program. There are useful Parent Handouts for each step. Sample Daily School Behavior Report Cards are included as well.

The Love and Logic Institute in Golden, Colorado has published an extensive number of parent training publications including:

Parenting With Love and Logic—Teaching Children Responsibility by Foster W. Cline, M. D., and Jim Fay. It is designed to help children "Learn to solve their own problems," and for parents to "Establish healthy control without resorting to anger . . . or exhausting power struggles."

Parenting Teens with Love and Logic—Preparing Adolescents for Responsible Adulthood by Foster W. Cline, M. D., and Jim Fay. The book is designed to "Provide parents with simple techniques and practical suggestions for dealing with key issues" in adolescents' lives.

You may contact the Love and Logic Institute at 1–800–338–4065. The internet address is www.loveandlogic.com.

1–2–3 Magic—Effective Discipline for Children 2–12 by Thomas W. Phelan, Ph.D., Child Management, Inc., Glen Ellyn, Illinois, 1995. In this book, Dr. Phelan aims to "Teach (parents) some very simple, precise and effective ways to manage children in the approximately two-to-twelve-year-old range." He focuses on *Stop Behaviors* such as arguing, fighting, tantrums, teasing and *Start Behaviors* such as doing homework, going to bed, cleaning rooms. The book provides clear statements of guidelines and provides many examples of applying the 1–2–3 method of discipline. The phone number is 1–800–442–4453.

SOS! Help for Parents by Lynn Clark, Ph.D., Parents Press, Bowling Green, Ky., 1985. This illustrated book is a parents' "Guide for handling a variety of common behavior problems." It includes "Fundamentals of Child Behavior and Effective Discipline, Basic Skills of the Time-Out Method" (this section is particularly useful) and use of points/tokens and behavioral contracts. The author includes tear-out sheets for parents and teachers.

Don Dinkmeyer and Gary D. McKay have published several good parenting books including *The Parent's Guide: Systematic Training for Effective Parenting (STEP)*, (1989). American Guidance Service, and *The Effective Parent*, (1987). American Guidance Service.

Dinkmeyer's STEP approach provides parent training in communication skills of effective listening, understanding children's behavior, and setting limits using natural and logical consequences.

HOW TO DO PARENT CONSULTATION TO MANAGE BEHAVIOR PROBLEMS

1. Identify the Problem(s)

In the first session, I ask the child if she knows why she came to see me. If a child is hesitant to talk, I say, "Children come to see me for different reasons. Sometimes it's because they are sad, mad, or afraid. Some come because they are having problems at home with their parents or brothers and sisters. Some are having trouble at school doing their work, or obeying teachers, or getting along with other children. Some have had some bad things happen to them or their family. Which kind of things have been bothering you?"

In the child's presence, I discuss the parents' main concerns. I want the child to know the reason she has come to see me.

2. Assess the Problem.

Determine whether the problem needs a medical referral, whether a medication assessment may be needed and what therapies, in addition to behavior therapy, are warranted.

3. Determine Target Behaviors

With the parents' input, I state the two or three target behaviors for beginning therapy. Parents may state the problem only in "don't" terms, or in overgeneralities such as, "He *never* minds me," "She's *always* fighting with her little sister," or "He's *always* in trouble at school." I ask parents to be specific in stating target behaviors. Example: For Benjamin to control hitting, kicking, and pushing at school (see Chapter 11).

This is the information I seek from parents (and from the child if she is able/willing to respond) to develop and implement a behavior management plan.

Information to be gathered regarding target behaviors include:

- Frequency: How often do they occur?
- Severity level.
- Setting: Where does this behavior occur most often?

4. Parents' Profile
- What are the mother's and father's parenting styles?

- In what areas do they agree/disagree regarding parenting?
- How consistent are parents in their discipline?

5. Family Rules
   - What are the main family rules?

6. Rewards and Punishment Inventory
   - For the child, what are the important material, social, and activity rewards?
   - What kind of punishment is most effective with this child?
   - With parents, develop a menu of rewards and punishments to use in their behavior management plan.

7. Start with a realistic goal. Pick at least one behavior to work on. Have the parents write out target behavior(s) with positive and negative consequences for the child. Have the parents explain the plan to the child.

8. Implement the Child Management Plan
   - Use behavior therapy principles presented in Chapter 11, *Guidelinesfor Behavior Management.*
   - Record keeping. Have the parents keep a daily/ weekly record of behavior. Review with the child at each session.
   - With the child, review the goals, teach new behaviors, reinforce positive steps.
   - Adapt the plan to this particular child. Make adjustments to the plan based on feedback about what is and what is not effective.

- Be consistent and persistent. It takes several weeks to develop new habits.
9. Look for generalizations of behavior to other settings.
10. Provide followup at one- and two-month intervals. Suggest booster sessions if needed.

Case Example of a Parent Consultation

Kerry, age five, diagnosis of Attention Deficit Hyperactivity Disorder and Adjustment Disorder with Disturbance of Emotions and Conduct.

Kerry was an only child who lived with his biological parents. His father had a history of depression and ADHD and was under psychiatric care.

1. Identify the Problem(s).
   - ADHD: impulsive, hyperactive behavior.
   - Aggressive behavior at day care and at home.
   - Noncompliance/resistance to parents' rules.
2. Assess whether a medical referral or additional therapies are needed.

Kerry's ADHD diagnosis was confirmed by observation, an interview with parents, and parent and teacher ADHD checklists. I referred Kerry to his pediatrician for a medication assessment.

3. Determine Target Behaviors:

	Frequency			
	H	D	W	M*
a) Hyperactivity and and distractibility		X		
b) Noncompliance (disobeying)		X		
c) Aggressive Behavior	X			

	Severity Level			
	M	M	S	VS**
a) Hyperactivity and Distractibility		X		
b) Noncompliance (disobeying)		X		
c) Anger Behavior		X		

Where: Most frequent setting? At home and at day care.

When: Time most likely to occur? Kerry's ADHD behavior problems occurred most often when he was in a public setting. Noncompliance (disobeying) occurred at home when he was told to stop playing and get ready for day care, or put toys away. Anger behavior occurred most often when he lost in a video game or when he was told "No" by his mother.

*H = Hourly; D = Daily; W = Weekly; M = Monthly
**M = Mild; M = Moderate; S = Severe; VS = Very Severe

4. Parenting Styles: Strict? Lenient? Democratic? In-
    dulgent? Aloof? Affectionate? Other?

    Mother: Democratic. Father: Aloof.
    Specific areas of similarities in parenting styles?
    Both Kerry's mother and father saw the need for
clear limits and for parent affection.
    Specific areas of differences in parenting styles?
    Mother was involved daily in rules and with af-
fection. She was more democratic in her approach,
but felt helpless to manage Kerry when he resisted.
Father was less involved in daily activities with Kerry
and he was inconsistent in showing affection.
    How are differences handled?
    Mother usually took care of the situation and
father became less involved.

5. List the Main Family Rules.
    • To help dress self for day care.
    • To put toys away when finished playing with
      them.
    • To obey mother and father when told to do a
      task.
    • Not to hit or fight with other children.
    • To obey his day care teachers.

6. Reinforcement (rewards) and Punishment Inven-
    tory.
    • Kerry's favorite material rewards: Ice cream,
      computer games, *Nintendo* toys.
    • Kerry's favorite activities: Computer games,

video games, war games, free play time, being
read to, sand tray play, drawing.
- Kerry's favorite social rewards: Attention from
his mother, father or maternal grandmother.
- Effective punishment: Loss of freedom, loss of
video games, time out.
7. Realistic goal(s): Reduce the three target behaviors of hyperactivity and distractibility, disobeying, and anger behavior.
8–10. Implement plan, look for generalizations, provide follow up.

Four sessions were required to develop and implement the behavior plan. Play therapy provided an
outlet for controlled aggression and for Kerry's sadness and anxiety related to his father's health problems.

The behavior management treatment reduced
ADHD behavior so that medication was postponed
until Kerry entered kindergarten, if needed at that
time. Impulsive and aggressive behavior problems
were reduced from hourly to an average of one every
two days. Kerry showed significant improvement in
the morning routine of getting ready for day care. He
resisted his mother less, but he still had difficulty
minding her two to three days each week.

I saw Kerry for six months. When he received
satisfactory behavior reports from day care, preschool,
and home for four consecutive weeks, his treatment
was terminated.

Summary of plan's effectiveness:

The plan was moderately effective in meeting the three target behavior goals.

PRACTICAL EXERCISE

Conduct a parent consultation to manage a child's difficult behavior using the format in Appendix 8.

Afterword

Before writing this book, I asked myself "What knowledge have I gained in over twenty-five years of working with children? Do I have something worthwhile to share with other child therapists?"

I determined to summarize what I have experienced; to recall the rewarding, challenging, and unique privileges I have had in treating children.

So, I decided we would write this handbook. First, for myself to record my memories and, second, with the assumption that we had something to share. This was our intent in writing the book. We have accomplished the first. You will have to decide about the second.

Max Price, Ph.D.

Appendix 1

CENTER FOR COUNSELING AND CARE OF OKLAHOMA, INC.

INFORMED CONSENT, DESCRIPTION OF SERVICES, AND CONFIDENTIALITY

Description of Services: It is my understanding that _____
is a _____ therapist. Counseling and psychotherapy involve discussing in detail my concerns, giving background information, and talking about areas of my life that may cause me emotional pain, all for the purpose of trying to develop new and more effective methods of coping with problem areas in my (or my child's) life. I understand that I am free to withdraw from therapeutic contact at any time if I so desire, and will only be responsible to pay for the completed sessions.

Confidentiality: All services rendered and all information obtained are kept confidential and cannot be released without your permission. You need to know however, that there are special situations under which confidential information could be revealed such as:

1. A "Duty to Warn" and "Duty to Protect" ethic allows a clinician to break confidentiality when a danger exists to the client and/or others.

2. Under very special circumstances, the court may subpoena a client's records, and may order a clinician to give testimony during a court hearing.

3. Third party payors, such as insurance companies, have a right to review a client's records prior to payment.

Your signature indicates that you have read and understand the above information concerning confidentiality, and that you have read and understand the description of services, and consent is given to provide services to you and/or your child (or children) _____ who is (are) not of legal age.

Your fee will be $____.00 per session. Sessions are 45 minutes. Payment of services is expected at the time services are provided unless arrangements are made prior to the appointment.

_____   _____   _____
Signature   Date   Relationship if client
                                     is a minor

_____   _____
Witness   Date

Appendix 2

DESCRIPTION OF CHILD

_____

_____

_____

_____

Table 2–7   Assessment of Needs

	Low	Average	High	Very High
For Structure				
For Limits				
For Control				
For Freedom				
For Security				
For Emotional Support (nurturing, affection)				
For Anger Management				
For Impulse Control				

SUMMARY OF NEEDS

_____

_____

_____

_____

Table 2–8   Assessing Developmental Levels

Chronological Age	
Physical Stature	
Cognitive Level	
Social/Emotional	

DEVELOPMENTAL LEVEL SUMMARY

_____

_____

_____

_____

Table 2–9   Core Conflicts Rating

	Satisfactory Coping	Minor Conflict	Major Conflict
Dependence versus Independence			
Security versus Anxiety			
Aggression and its Control			
Love versus Hate			
Sensual Pleasure and its Renunciation			
Excitement versus Boredom			

CORE CONFLICTS SUMMARY

TREATMENT PLAN

_____

_____

_____

_____

Appendix 3

MOST IMPORTANT TOYS

What if you are just beginning to equip your office for play therapy? What if you travel to several locations and need to provide a traveling play therapy room? What are the essential toys to provide? I recommend:

1. A dollhouse with toy furniture and people.
2. Modeling clay, toy animals, and people.
3. Puppets
4. Drawing materials including markets, colored pencils,and crayons.
5. Tape recorder.
6. Games for younger children such as *Candyland*.
7. Games for older children such as *Thinking, Feeling, Doing* (1973) game.

Appendix 4

CHILD REINFORCEMENT INVENTORY

Questions to ask a child if he or she is old enough to respond:

1. What things do you like to do?
2. Who do you like to spend time with?
3. When you do something good, what do you like to hear your Mom (Dad, caregiver) say?
4. What thing would you like to have that doesn't cost a lot of money (monetary reward)? What special activity would you like to do (privilege to earn)?
5. What is someting you really dislike having to do?
6. What is something you would like to learn?

Questions to ask the parent(s)/caregivers:

1. What things does your child like to do?
2. Who does your child like to spend time with?
3. When your child does something good, what does she/he like to hear you say?

4. What is something you think your child would
   like to have that doesn't cost a lot of money?
5. What privilege do you think your child would like
   to earn?
6. What kinds of punishment have worked with your
   child in the past?
7. What kinds of punishment have not worked?
8. What is something you think your child would be
   interested in learning?

Appendix 5

Daily Home Behavior Report Card

Child's name _____ Date _____

Parents:
Please rate your child's behavior today in the ares listed below. Use a separate column for each subject. Use the following ratings: 1 = Excellent; 2 = Good; 3 = Fair; 4 = Poor and 5 = Very Poor. Then initial the box at the bottom of your column. Add any comments about your child's behavior today on the back of this card.

	Time Period				
Behaviors to be rated	**4 p.m.**	**5 p.m.**	**6 p.m.**	**7 p.m.**	**8 p.m.**
1)					
2)					
3)					
Parent's initials					

Appendix 6

Daily School Behavior Report Card

Child's name _____ Date _____

Teachers:
Please rate this child's behavior today in the ares listed below. Use a separate column for each subject or class period. Use the following ratings: 1 = Excellent; 2 = Good; 3 = Fair; 4 = Poor and 5 = Very Poor. Then initial the box at the bottom of your column. Add any comments about the child's behavior today on the back of this card.

Time Period

Behaviors to be rated	9 a.m.	10 a.m.	11 a.m.	Lunch	1 p.m.	2 p.m.	3 p.m.
1)							
2)							
3)							
Teacher's initials							

Appendix 7

GUIDELINES FOR BEHAVIOR MANAGEMENT

When you wish to change a child's behavior, you have four choices:

1. **Reward behavior** when you like what the child is doing. Use positive reinforcement.
2. **Ignore behavior** when you don't like what the child is doing.
3. **Punish behavior** that you can't ignore. Use aversive consequences.
4. **Teach new behavior** when you want the child to learn new responses. Use modeling and imitation learning.

Principles of Behavior Management

The focus is on behavior—**learned** behavior.

1. To **increase** a particular behavior, use **positive reinforcement** (reward).

Positive reinforcer: Anything that increases the likelihood that a behavior will be repeated.

Primary (unlearned) reinforcers: Food, water, air. (Example: A favorite snack for satisfactory behavior.)

Secondary (learned) reinforcers: Attention, praise, privilege, success, money.

Attention from an adult is a powerful reinforcer for most children. (Example: Praise for completing a chore.)

2. Rewarding improvements leads to further improvements (shaping). (Example: A child praised for helping an adult put her toys away, then praised for putting toys away on her own.)

3. Reward immediately (as quickly as possible). Small immediate rewards are more powerful than large, delayed rewards.

4. Begin with frequent rewards to establish behavior, then move to occasional rewards to maintain behavior. (Example: A child receives praise and a token for not hitting for one hour. With improvement, move the child to every two hours, and then reward for maintaining the behavior for an entire day.)

5. Reward consistently. Work for 95% to 100% consistency by caregivers. Without consistency, behavior is not likely to improve.

6. To teach new behavior, use *modeling* (imitation learning) as in "Monkey see, monkey do," and practice (behavioral rehearsal).

Modeling (imitation learning) is a source of positive and negative learning.

Positive example: When an adult expresses frustration clearly by telling the child:

"I'm angry at you because you hit Jimmy."

Negative example: Yelling when mad.

Behavior rehearsal: Have child practice the behavior you have demonstrated.

Example: Showing a child how to catch a ball and practicing with the child.

7. To reduce a behavior, use ignoring (non-reward). (Example: Not giving attention when the child interrupts but using hand gesture to show "stop." Thank the child for waiting and then give attention.)

8. To reduce a behavior, use an effective punishment (when behavior cannot be ignored). Punishment should be administered consistently without strong anger and with the least possible amount of talking.

    *Time out (loss of freedom). The rule of thumb is a one-minute timeout for each year of age. (Example: A six-year-old child is given a six-minute time out for throwing a toy across the room.)

    *Overcorrection (repeating a corrective activity). (Example: Child is required to wash and rewash the floor three times after he tracks mud into the house.)

(Example: Child who runs down the hall is required to practice walking down the hall slowly three times. This is behavior rehearsal of the desired behavior.)

Appendix 8

PARENT CONSULTATION— CHILD MANAGEMENT GUIDELINES

PRACTICAL EXERCISE

Conduct a parent consultation to manage a child's difficult behavior using the following format:

1. Identify the Problem(s).

2. Assess whether a medical referral or additional therapies are needed.

3. Determine Target Behaviors.

	Frequency			
	H	*D*	*W*	*M**
a) _____ _____.	___	___	___	___
b) _____ _____.	___	___	___	___
c) _____ _____.	___	___	___	___

	Severity Level			
	M	*M*	*S*	*VS***
a) Target Behavior #1	___	___	___	___
b) Target Behavior #2	___	___	___	___
c) Target Behavior #4	___	___	___	___

Where: Most frequent setting?

When: Time most likely to occur?

4. Parenting Styles: Strict? Lenient? Democratic? Indulgent? Aloof? Affectionate?

Other?

Mother _____

Father _____

Specific areas of similarities in parenting styles?

*H = Hourly; D = Daily; W = Weekly; M = Monthly

**M = Mild; M = Moderate; S = Severe; VS = Very Severe

Specific areas of differences in parenting styles?

How are differences handled?
Compromise _____
Support each other's rules _____
Arguing _____
One parent takes charge _____
No resolution _____
Other _____

5. List main family rules:

   _____
   _____
   _____
   _____

6. Reinforcement (rewards) and Punishment Inventory:
   Favorite material rewards

   _____
   _____
   _____
   _____

   Favorite activities

   _____
   _____
   _____
   _____

Favorite social rewards:

_____

_____

_____

_____

Effective punishments:

_____

_____

_____

_____

7. Realistic Goal(s):
   Behavior One:

_____

_____

_____

_____

Behavior Two:

_____

_____

_____

_____

Behavior Three:

_____

_____

_____

_____

Chart Progress:

Child Management Plan:

8-10. Describe how the plan was implemented. Use record keeping and review   goals and behavior. Look for generalization of behaviors, provide follow up.

REFERENCES

Barkley, R.A., (1997). *Defiant Children—A Clinician's Manual for Assessment and Parent Training.* New York: Guilford Press.

Breger, Louis (1974). *From Instinct to Identity.* New Jersey: Prentice-Hall, Inc.

Brown, L.K., and M. (1986). *Dinosaur's Divorce.* Boston, New York, Toronto, London: Little, Brown and Company.

Clark, L. (1985). *SOS! Help for Parents.* Bowling Green, Kentucky: Parents Press.

Cline, F.W., and Fay, J. (1990). *Parenting with Love and Logic—Teaching Children Responsibility.* Colorado Springs, Colorado: Pinon Press.

Gardner, R.A. (1973). *The Talking, Feeling, and Doing Game.* Cresskill: Creative Therapeutics.

———. (1971b). *Therapeutic Communication with Children: The Mutual Storytelling Technique.* New York: Jason Aronson.

Handbook of Play Therapy (1983). Edited by Charles E. Schaefer and Kevin J. O'Connor. New York: John Wiley & Sons.

Keats, D.B. II, (1990). *Child Multimodal Therapy.* Norwood, NJ: Ablex Publishing Corporation.

Moss, D.M. (1989). *Shelley the Hyperactive Turtle.* USA: Woodbine House, Inc.

Phelan, T.W. (1995). *1–2–3 Magic—Effective Discipline for Children 2–12.* Glen Ellyn, Illinois: Child Management, Inc.

Stiles, N. (1984). *I'll Miss You, Mr. Hooper.* New York and Canada: Random House/Children's Television Workshop.

Zakich, R. (1975). *The Ungame.* Anaheim, CA: The Ungame Company.

INDEX

Adapting therapy in
  behavior therapy, 260
Adaptive functioning,
  higher, 39
ADDES Rating Forms, 21
Adjustment disorder
  with anxiety and
    depression, 126–134,
    185–186
  with disturbance of
    conduct, 141–144, 288
Adolescent onset, 164–169
Adoption, 200–201
  child dealing with foster
    care and, 202–206
Aggression, 42
  assessing aggression and
    its control, 23
  setting limits and
    physical, 9
  toys as symbols for, 81
  use of toys as outlets
    for, 76–77

American Red Cross, 226
Anxiety and depression,
  treatment of
  adjustment disorder
    with anxiety, 126–129
  adjustment disorder
    with anxiety and
    depression, 185–186
  assessing security vs.
    anxiety, 22
  child with depression,
    ADHD, and an
    absentee father, 182–
    185
  fears and anxiety,
    sadness/depression
    themes, 43
  multimodal therapy
    techniques for, 119–
    121, 122, 130, 135–
    136
  practical exercise, 138–
    139

Anxiety and depression
(continued)
separation anxiety, 24,
120–126, 136, 232,
234, 251, 267–268
treatment of anxiety,
121–129
treatment of depression,
5, 129–138
Assertive play, 25
Asthma, children with,
231–234
Attachment Disorder of
Early Childhood, 4, 54
Attachment issues, with
foster children, 201–
202
Attention Deficit Disorder
(ADD), 147
stories for children with,
113
Attention Deficit
Hyperactivity
Disorder (ADHD)
behavior management
approach for, 250,
261, 288, 291
child with cystic
fibrosis and, 240–241
child with depression,
ADHD, and an
absentee father, 182–
185

Oppositional Defiant
Disorder (ODD) and,
152–157
treatment of, 140, 147–
152
Audio and video tapes in
storytelling, use of,
77, 88, 111–112, 188–
189, 194, 195
Autism, behavior
management for, 253,
273
Autonomy, independence,
and freedom, toys as
symbols for, 83
Axline, Virginia, 41

Barkley, Russell A., 283
Barton, Sharon, 40–41
Basic assumptions about
play therapy, 37–38
child's developmental
level, 39
higher adaptive
functioning, 40
play therapy is a
specialized use of
play, 39
unstructured play, 38–39
Behavior checklists, 21
Behavior and emotional
problems, using play
for, 42–43

Behavior problems,
treatment of
adjustment disorder
with disturbance of
conduct, 141–144
Attention deficit
Hyperactivity
Disorder (ADHD),
147–157
childhood onset conduct
disorder, 158–163
child with seizure
disorder and behavior
problems, 236
conduct disorder-group
type, adolescent onset
and Dysthymia, 164–
169
conduct disorders,
157
learning disability and
ADHD, 150–152
Oppositional Defiant
Disorder (ODD), 144–
147, 152–157
practical exercise, 169–
171
See also Managing
difficult behavior;
Parent consultation
for managing behavior
problems
Behavior rehearsal, 256

Behavior report card
daily home, 305
daily school, 307
Behavior therapy
managing difficult
behavior and
applying, 257–261
in multimodal approach,
122
using play with, 43–44
Bell's Palsy, 242
Bibliotherapy, 112–113,
149, 180, 188
Bosnian children, victims
of war, 214, 223–226
Brazelton, T. Berry, 38
Breger, Louis, 22

Cancer/tumors, children
with, 242–244
Chance Level stage of play,
42
Characteristics of an
effective play
therapist, 45
ability to play with
children, 46
belief in the efficacy of
play therapy, 47
good facilitation skills,
48
knowledge of child
development, 46

Characteristics of an effective play therapist *(continued)*
  a sound theoretical foundation, 46
  uses the scientific method in therapy, 47
Childhood onset conduct disorder, 158–163
Child Multimodal Therapy (Keats), 119–120
Childquotes
  on being good, 276
  on birth control, 62
  child's insight, 86
  on child's understanding, 86
  complimenting mom, 246
  creative thinking, 50
  empathy of children, 115
  a forever family, 172
  guilty, not guilty, 140
  I don't need therapy, 276
  I got problems, 18
  more understanding; less advice, 172
  not to worry, 140
  the rewards I need, 212
  test responses, 36
  wanting to be big, 50
Child reinforcement inventory, 303–304

Child Symptom Inventory, 21
Chronic illnesses, children with, 231
  asthma, 231–234
  chronic pain, 237–238
  seizure disorder, 234–236
Clark, Lynn, 284–285
Client-centered play therapy, 53, 54, 55, 59
Cline, Foster W., 283–284
Cognitive-behavioral play therapy, 51, 54, 55, 57, 58–59, 122
Cognitive development model, Piaget's, 41
Conduct disorder-group type, adolescent onset and Dysthymia, 164–169
Conduct disorders, 157
Conducting a play therapy session
  how active should the therapist be?, 10–12
  how to assess the child's treatment needs in today's session, 7–8
  how to begin a play therapy session, 3–5
  how to end a session, 12–13
  how to establish rapport with a child, 5–7

how to give structure,
set limits, and allow
freedom, 9–10
how to include parents
and caregivers, 13–15
practical exercise, 15–
17
Confidentiality, child's
right to, 14, 296
Conners' Parent Rating
Scales, 21
Consistency in behavior
therapy, 259
Core conflicts, assessing,
22, 28–29, 34, 299
aggression and its
control, 23
dependence vs.
independence, 22
excitement vs. boredom,
23–24
love vs. hate, 23
security vs. anxiety, 22
sensual pleasure and its
renunciation, 23
Cystic fibrosis, children
with, 238–241

Danger or threat, toys as
symbols for, 81–82
Death of a family member,
186
child coping with death
of two siblings, 197–
199

child coping with
sudden death of
father, 192–197
child coping with
sudden death of
mother, 186–192
stories for children
coping with death,
112
Defiant Children—A
Clinician's Manual
for Assessment and
Parent Training
(Barkley), 283
Dependence, helplessness,
and weakness, toys as
symbols for, 82–83
Dependent play, 25–26
Depression. See anxiety
and depression,
treatment of
Destructive play, setting
limits and, 9
Developmental levels,
assessment of, 21, 27–
28, 33, 298
knowing a child's
development level, 39
Developmental play
theory, 51, 52–53, 54,
55, 57
Diagnostic assessment, 19
additional testing, 21
assessing core conflicts,
22–24

Diagnostic assessment
    (continued)
    for assessing needs, 43
    background
        information, 20
    behavioral and
        emotional problems,
        42–43
    behavior checklists, 21
    diagnostic interview,
        20–21
    diagnostic play (two
        sessions), 21–24
    previous testing, 20
    social/emotional levels,
        40–42
Diagnostic play, 19
    case examples, 24–35
    diagnostic assessment,
        19–24
    practical exercise, 35
Differential reinforcement,
    265
Dinkmeyer, Don, 285
Dinosaur's Divorce (Brown
    and Brown), 113, 180
Divorce
    anxiety and children
        coping with, 126–129
    child facing parents'
        divorce, 176–179
    stories for children
        coping with, 113
    visitation problems, and
        blended families, 179–
        182

Dysthymia, 135–138, 164–
    169

Elkind, David, 53
Empathy, 6–7
Encopresis, 158
Ending play therapy
    sessions, 12–13
Erikson, Erik, 41, 53

Fears and anxiety,
    sadness/depression
    themes, 43
Foster care, 201–202
    child dealing with foster
        care and adoption,
        202–206
    child in long-term foster
        care, with a
        developmental
    disability and a thought
        disorder, 206–208
Freedom in play therapy,
    allowing, 9–10
Free play, 39
From Instinct to Identity
    (Breger), 22

Games, 78
    Candyland, 41–42, 79,
        205, 301
    Carrom, 31, 79
    chance games, 78–79
    outdoor games, 80
    skill games, 79
    Sorry, 31, 79

therapeutic games, 31,
79–80, 239
*Thinking, Feeling,
Doing Game*, 31, 79–
80, 122, 301
Ungame, 80
Gardner, Richard A., 31,
79–80, 88–90
Gesell Institute of Human
Development, 52–53
Ginott, Haim, 37
Grief therapy, 175, 186,
197

*Handbook of Play
Therapy* (Schaefer and
O'Connor), 51, 88–89
Hawthorne Educational
Services, Inc., 21
Heart disease, children
with, 241–242
"Helping Children Cope
with Disaster"
(pamphlet), 226
House-Tree-Person
Drawing Test, 20, 31,
69, 70–71

I'll Miss You, Mr. Hooper
(Stiles), 112, 188
Informed Consent, 14–15,
296

James, O'Dessie Oliver,
51–52

Keats, Donald, 119–120
Kinetic Family Drawing,
20, 31, 69, 137, 251,
266

Learned behavior, 254–255
Learning disability,
Attention Deficit
Hyperactivity
Disorder (ADHD) and,
150–152
Life threatening illnesses,
children with cancer/
tumors, 242–244
cystic fibrosis, 238–241
heart disease, 241–242
Limit setting in play
therapy, 9–10, 13
behavior therapy and
limit setting/rules,
258–259
Lying behavior, 252

McKay, Gary D., 285
Managing difficult
behavior, 249
applying behavior
therapy, 257–275
description and
intervention, 249–253
guidelines for behavior
management, 254–
256, 309–312
practical exercise, 275–
276

Managing difficult
behavior *(continued)*
principles of behavior
management, 254–
256, 309–312
Modeling (imitation
learning), 255
Multimodal approach
in children experiencing
separation and loss,
173–174
in treatment of anxiety
and depression, 119–
121, 122, 130, 135–
136
in treatment of behavior
problems, 141–169
Mutual storytelling
case example, 91–94
for children coping with
death, 188–189
continuous story
variation of, 94, 98–
103, 130–134
fill-in-the-blanks story
variation of, 94, 103–
106
Gardner's technique,
88–90
"I'll tell you a story"
variation of, 94–98
in treating behavior
problems, 162–163
variations of, 94–106

Natural disasters (storms,
fire, floods), 226
children's common
reactions following a
disaster, 226–228
tornado victim, 229–230
Needs, assessment of, 21,
25–27, 30–32, 43,
297–298
behavior therapy and, 257
Nighttime fears/terrors,
27, 237, 121.221
Nurturing, toys as
symbols for, 82

O'Connor, Kevin, 39, 51,
89
Oklahoma City bombing,
victims of the, 213,
219–222
*1-2-3 Magic—Effective
Discipline for
Children 2–12*
(Phelan), 284
Oppositional Defiant
Disorder (ODD), 144–
147
Attention Deficit
Hyperactivity
Disorder (ADHD) and,
152–157
behavior therapy and
oppositional defiant
behavior, 264, 270

Overcorrection, behavior
management and,
256

Parent Child Interaction
Training (PCIT), 44–
45
Parent consultation for
managing behavior
problems, 277–278
assumptions about child
management, 278–283
case example of a parent
consultation, 288–292
how to do parent
consultation to
manage behavior
problems, 285–292
practical exercises, 292,
313–317
resources, 283–285
*Parenting Teens with Love
and Logic—Preparing
Adolescents for
Responsible
Adulthood* (Cline),
284
*Parenting With Love and
Logic—Teaching
Children
Responsibility*
(Cline), 283–284
Parents/caregivers
absentee parent, 182–186

how to include, 13–15
in treating stressed
children, 175–176
using play as a means of
teaching how to
parent, 44–45
*Parent's Guide: Systemic
Training for Effective
Parenting (STEP), The*
(Dinkmeyer and
McKay), 285
Phelan, Thomas W., 284
Piaget, J., 41
*Play Therapy: A
Comprehensive
Guide* (James), 51–52
Play therapy materials. *See*
Toys in play therapy
Play therapy model,
Axline's, 41
Play Therapy Primer, The
(O'Connor), 51
Play in therapy, uses of,
40
with behavior therapy,
43–44
in diagnostic
assessment, 40–43
as a means of teaching
how to parent, 44–45
with preschool and
elementary school age
children, 45
for rapport building, 43

Post-Traumatic Stress Disorder (PTSD), 214–215

Power and mastery, toys as symbols for, 83–84

Pseudo-attachments, children forming, 201–202

Psycho-dynamic play therapy, 55, 57

Psychosocial theory, Erikson's, 41

Rapport
  establishing rapport with a child, 5–7
  using play for building, 43

Record keeping/compliance in behavior therapy, 259–260

Regression, 42

Rehearsal play, 217

Reinforcement history in behavior therapy, 258

Rewarding behavior improvements, 255

Roberts Apperception Test for Children (RATC), 31, 34

Rogers, Carl, 53

Safety and protection, toys as symbols for, 82

Sand tray play, 72
  for children coping with death, 194–195
  for children coping with divorce, 180
  for chronic pain sufferers, 237
  for trauma victims, 216, 217–218
  in treating anxiety, 122–123
  for victims of natural disasters, 229–230

Scales of Independent Behavior—Revised (SIB-R), 274

Schaefer, Charles E., 51, 89

Seizure disorders, children suffering from, 234–236

Self control in behavior therapy, 260–261

Sentence completion test, 20, 236 .

Separation anxiety, 24, 120–126, 136, 232, 234, 251, 267–268

Separation and loss, play therapy applied to, 173–174
  absentee parent, 182–186
  adoption, 200–201
  death of a family member, 186–199
  divorce, 176–182

foster care, 201-208
guidelines for treating
stressed children,
174–176
practical exercise, 208–211
typical treatment plan,
174
Setting limits in play
therapy, 9–10, 13
behavior therapy and,
258–259
Severely emotionally
disturbed (SED),
classes for the, 153,
161, 162, 183
Shelley, the Hyperactive
Turtle (Moss), 113,
140, 149
Skill Level stage of play,
42
Social/emotional levels,
using play for
revealing, 40–42
SOS! Help for Parents
(Clark), 284–285
Stages of play, 41–42
State-Trait Anxiety
Inventory for
Children (STAIC),
121–122
Storytelling, therapeutic,
68, 87–88
bibliotherapy, 112–113,
149, 180, 188

for children coping with
death, 188–189, 194,
195–196
for children coping with
divorce, 177–178
a child's life story, 109–111
mutual storytelling, 88–105
practical exercise, 113–114
storytelling as part of
play activities, 106–109
for trauma victims, 216,
225–226
in treating anxiety, 122,
123–126
in treating behavior
problems, 162–163
in treating depression,
130–134
use of audio and video
tapes, 111–112
Stress management, 45,
173
guidelines for treating
stressed children,
174–176
Structured play, 39
Structure in play therapy,
giving, 9–10
Symbolic play, 217, 230
Systems theory, 51, 57,
59

Talk therapy, 43, 177
Theoretical orientations in play therapy, 51–52
   case examples, 54–59
   development theory, 52–53
   necessary conditions for therapeutic change, 53–54
   practical exercise, 59–61
   theory in practice, 54–59
Therapeutic Communication with Children—The Mutual Storytelling Technique (Gardner), 88
Thinking, Feeling, Doing Game, 31, 79–80, 122, 301
Time out (loss of freedom), 256
Toys in play therapy, 37–38, 65
   building materials, 72–73
   chance games, 78–79
   clay, 67–68, 216
   dollhouse with furniture and doll families, 66
   dolls and stuffed animals, 74
   drawing materials, 69–71

   games, 78–81
   most important, 301
   outdoor games, 80–81
   play doctor's kit, 77, 235
   practical exercise, 85–86
   puppets, 74–75, 221, 235
   sand tray, 72
   skill games, 79
   symbols that toys represent for children, 81–84
   tape recorder, 77
   telephones (toy phones), 75
   therapeutic games, 79–80
   toy animals, 68
   toy guns, 76–77
   toy people, 68–69
   toy vehicles, 73–74
   wonder toys, 78
Trauma and illness, play therapy applied to
   chronic illness, 231–238
   life threatening illness, 238–244
   natural disasters, 226–230
   practical exercise, 244–246
   violence, 213–226

Ungame, 80
Unstructured play, 38–39

Violence, victims of, 213–
    215
  Bosnian children, victims
    of war, 223–226
  child in fatal car
    collision, 216–219
  death of day care
    classmates, 221–222
  death of mother from
    act of terrorism, 219–
    221

treatment guidelines,
    215–216
victims of neglect and
    abuse, 222–223

Win Level stage of play,
    41, 72–73, 78, 229
Win/Win Level stage of
    play, 41–42, 72–73,
    78, 205

ABOUT THE AUTHORS

B. Max Price received his Ph.D. in Counseling Psychology from the University of Oklahoma, Norman. Specializing in child psychology, Dr. Price has been in group private practice since 1977 with Behavioral Medicine Associates (1977–1993), and Integris Baptist Medical Center Outpatient Counseling (1993–1998). Since 1998, he has practiced with the Center for Counseling and Care of Oklahoma, Inc. He has served on the Board of Directors of the Oklahoma Psychological Association and is a member of the American Psychological Association and the National Register of Psychologists. He is the author of two books, numerous publications and magazine articles on child guidance, parenting, children in crisis, and children and stress.

Geri Price received her bachelor's degree in Business from Oklahoma City University. She has been a Senior Consultant for the Center for Nonprofit Management, working with dozens of organizations in Strategic Planning. She has published several magazine articles. She currently works for the Oklahoma County Metropolitan Library System coordinating afterschool and summer reading programs for high-risk/low-income elementary school children.

The Price's have two children, Tracey and Todd, and four grandchildren.